knapsacking abroad

Herb and Judy Klinger

knapsacking
abroad

STACKPOLE BOOKS

Harrisburg, Pennsylvania

KNAPSACKING ABROAD

Copyright © 1967 by
STACKPOLE COMPANY
Cameron and Kelker Streets, Harrisburg, Pa. 17105

Price: $2.95

Printed in U.S.A.

Library of Congress Catalog Card Number: 67-13933

All rights reserved, including the right to reproduce this book or portions thereof in any form or by any means, electronic or mechanical, including photocopying, recording, or by any information storage and retrieval system, without permission in writing from the publisher. All inquiries should be addressed to The Stackpole Company, Cameron and Kelker Streets, Harrisburg, Pennsylvania 17105.

Dedicated to Helen and H. E. R. D., good travelers

CONTENTS

INTRODUCTION

INTRODUCTION

Knapsacking abroad is the trim, in-depth, least expensive means for seeing any part of the world. The bite of the travel bug is fatal only when the victim never gets around to indulging his fever. Escape? Why not? It's your world. Travel *is* an escape ... from a particular pattern of demands and routines to a consideration of life itself.

Our knapsacks carry the faint dust of 87 countries. Beyond the international facades of capital cities we observed life from the benches and baggage racks of vintage trains; joined the family scene from Kenyan manyatta to Balinese compound; relaxed on a Kashmiri houseboat; visited Fujiyama, Everest, Kilimanjaro; trekked in the Himalayas, Alps, and Andes. These knapsacks also made possible a bouncing trip overland from Europe to the East; sailing in the West Indies; wandering through the Black Forest; exploring behind the Iron Curtain; hitchhiking in Africa; camping along the Pan American Highway in Alaska and through Central America. They've taken us to Laos, Vietnam, the Congo, and made the pilgrimage to Auschwitz and Hiroshima. We tied our knapsacks to the magic carpets of the jet age, turning our backs, whenever possible, from vapor to adventure trails.

Flicking the dust off the knack of knapsackery revives the spirit of Polo, Franck, Halliburton. Here's what you'll need for the basic approach to travel. "Happiness is not a destination but a way of traveling." Happy wandering within, and beyond these covers.

CHAPTER 1

ANSWERS TO QUESTIONS ABOUT KNAPSACK TRAVEL

Knapsack travel is the classical high road to finding and living new worlds of people and ideas. It's roaming simply, discovering the revitalizing pleasure of being independent. Knapsacking allows you to go farther, see, and do more while concentrating on what you've come to experience that's not in your home neighborhood. It ties travel's latest technology to the money-saving, soul-stretching, grass-roots approach of "Das Wandern." You ride the sciences, but apply the arts.

WHY A KNAPSACK?

Weigh an empty suitcase. A knapsack is pounds lighter. Its tough construction endures back road bumps and tumbles. It'll squish under a train seat, provide a foot rest, or serve as a cushion. It expands or shrinks with your cubic needs. Outside pockets permit quick access to water bottle, raincoat, toothbrush. Compared with that Western box designed to encase suits, the knapsack, and all it represents, offers global versatility.

WHAT DOES IT REPRESENT?

Call it "knapsax-appeal." The knapsack spells adventure and frees you from a number of otherwise inhibiting pressures. It identifies you as a certain kind of traveler. Your scholastic days may be a hazy alumni memory. But locals read you as a student of the world, according you allowances traditionally reserved for students and seekers. People are friendly, because they consider you more approachable.

ARE THERE OTHER ADVANTAGES?

A knapsack guarantees greater mobility and forces you to travel light. It rests as a balanced and unconscious extension of your anatomy, leaving your hands free to shuffle tickets and passport, to catch a surreptitious photo, or peel a few bananas while sprinting for the morning lorry. It also takes naturally to mountains and byways through remote villages.

A knapsack smoothes your way. Thieves are out for richer pluckings. Tourist leeches classify you as "knowing the ropes" and head for other prey. Customs officials just smile and mark your gear with a sweep of the chalk, seldom bothering to inspect below the flap.

HOW EXPENSIVE IS KNAPSACK TRAVEL?

It's the least expensive of all travel. You're steered away from expensive hotels to the more practical hostelries. Hotel keepers eye the bag and tend to offer the most reasonable room. Strangers want you as their guest. You save cash by carrying, since the pack acts as vinegar, not honey, to a buzzing swarm of porters.

Ideas and initiative stretch further than money. Travel's central purposes and most of its attractions are free, or close to it. The major budget items— lodging, food, transport— the knapsacker can do something about. Without exception, it's cost us less to knapsack abroad than live at home. Many a luxury not easily permissible here is possible elsewhere, if, by avoiding the artificially inflated world of "tourist services," you stay within local economies where people meet the same human needs at a fraction of our own costs.

Some knapsackers manage to circumnavigate the globe for less than others spend in two weeks at Miami. You can comfortably sail around the world for as little as $756* on the M.S. "Australis," the former "America," although we've met pack-toting globetrotters who've done it on smaller sums. From New York, it's possible to fly with snorkel and flipper-eared pack to the Virgin Islands for less, including airfare, than an all-expense bus trip to Washington and Williamsburg. A week's

---

*Prices of goods and travel mentioned in this book may vary slightly because of inflationary pressures, fluctuation in foreign exchange rates, etc.

cruise down the upper Amazon comes to $4.50, meals included. Add round-trip fare of $180 from Miami, and who can afford to stay at home?

Pare to essentials. A typical travel agency's offerings usually differ from what you really need. Why seek the services of a yacht broker when you can paddle your own canoe, and a canoe will do? And we haven't yet discussed knapsacking campers and hitchhikers, who travel practically free.

IS THIS SOMETHING NEW FOR AMERICANS?

Yes. With increasing global sophistication, Americans are developing into a new breed of traveler. This prototype has learned from the frugal European, the ingenious student, from reading, returning travelers, overseas workers, and a good dose of foreign films as well, that familiar procedures hold true anywhere. Using common sense and an extra ounce of initiative to beat through the smoke screen of mythical monsters (which are some agents' stock in trade), he roams where and when he wishes. He combines an involvement with people and the local way of doing things with a maximum use of limited resources. With or without a knapsack, his approach, in growing numbers, is in the knapsack tradition.

JUST WHO IS THE KNAPSACK TRAVELER?

A renegade from the commuter dash, the housewife hop, the lawn-mower trot? Perhaps. More often knapsackers are college men and women, Peace Corps volunteers, or discharged servicemen taking the long way home...a graduate student who must clamber over every last classical ruin...a psychologist investigating voodoo death...a collector of aborigine pottery...a florist studying jungle orchids...two nurses on holiday...a professional man taking a "break"...a teacher's family on sabbatical...Germans, Japanese, Australians by the shipload, Americans, and, we swear on our passports, so help us American Express, an eighty-year-old great-grandmother.

ISN'T THIS THE BEATNIK
WAY OF TRAVEL?

It's the Halliburton, *wanderjahr* way of travel. The heroically shouldered bag identifies you as the most sophisticated of travelers. You're independent. You have time. You'll be asked, and will find that you can answer, a tourist's anxious questions about when, where, how, and how much. The knapsack traveler relies on his own resources, sharing, not trading on the good nature of those he meets. One young footloose backpacker when asked, "Doesn't the weight bend you over?", replied, "Maybe at first, only you quickly get used to it. Then, and maybe for the rest of your life, you stand a little taller."

DOES KNAPSACKING
REQUIRE CAMPING?

If you wish. Its versatility includes camping, even hitchhiking—if you wish. Knapsacking doesn't mean walking around the world—unless you want to. When you do walk, it's minus porters and pulled muscles.

WON'T I LOOK STRANGE
CARRYING A KNAPSACK?

The knapsack abroad is a respectable mark of the non-tourist traveler. In Africa your knapsack may cause good-natured laughter because, quite obviously, the load would be so much lighter if distributed on the spinal column from above. Your practical pack may arouse curiosity, envy. But it's always accepted.

IS KNAPSACK TRAVEL SAFE?

Safer than being a tourist. You blend. You belong. See Chapter 8.

IS KNAPSACKING
FOR THE FIRST-TIME TRAVELER?

Is travel value? You could join a tour to start, but will probably want to strike out on your own far more quickly than you now imagine.

IS IT BETTER TO TRAVEL ALONE?

"Start-alones" seldom stay alone unless that's the way they want it. Fortunate it is when you have a long-haul mate with whom to share travel's unified impact. More frequently this happens with kindred souls along the way. Often a growing compatibility with yourself leaves you in the finest company. This discovery is one of travel's greatest rewards. Girls may travel more adventurously as a pair.

WHERE ARE THE BEST PLACES TO TRAVEL WITH KNAPSACK?

God's clear blue sky covers all the world. It's your oyster. See Chapter 7.

DO I REALLY NEED A KNAPSACK?

Knapsacking is essentially a state of mind. It's a means of getting about that requires less dollars and cents and more everyday gumption and horse sense. It involves visiting places not exclusively pleasant, but always interesting. Not bound by iron-clad itineraries, the jet-knapsack set is outward bound to find its own.

With or without pack, it means being flexible enough to take things as they come, making the most of what's at hand. This requires an optimistic confidence that in each place things will work out, because, in looking back, they almost always have. When they haven't, there's the memory of exhilarating new experience.

WHY GO?

As if you didn't know! Modern homogenized life requires that we create our own antidotal adventures. Knapsacking lets us escape the limitations of a particular mold for continued new stimulation and personal growth. Our age makes it possible.

SO WHEN IS BEST?

Travel is an investment in yourself. Borrowing time from retirement adds quality to the years till then. Going "off-season" has obvious advantages, but is a tourist concept. The ideal time for knapsacking is whenever you can go.

CHAPTER 2

BATTLE PLAN FOR TAKEOFF

Travel reality comes from scrapping impulsive approaches for a deliberative one. Where to go, what to see—and do—depend on why you'd like to be off.

CONSTRUCTING A COUNT-DOWN CHART

Travel desires, once defined, reveal direction. When further translated into concrete goals, you get an idea of what it's going to take. Connect your present status with your goals through an unbroken staircase of readiness steps. Each step becomes an intermediate goal of its own. Intermediate goals tell us what must be done to be off. Each should follow the last, and lead easily to the next. Arrange yours in logical order. For example:

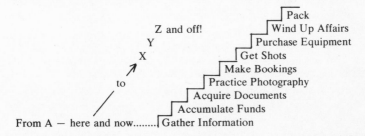

Once you've determined the *what's* for an ordered progression of steps, next list under each the specific tasks which explain *how*. Portions of a final plan might emerge as follows:

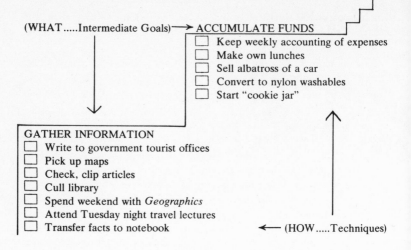

(WHAT.....Intermediate Goals) → ACCUMULATE FUNDS
☐ Keep weekly accounting of expenses
☐ Make own lunches
☐ Sell albatross of a car
☐ Convert to nylon washables
☐ Start "cookie jar"

GATHER INFORMATION
☐ Write to government tourist offices
☐ Pick up maps
☐ Check, clip articles
☐ Cull library
☐ Spend weekend with *Geographics*
☐ Attend Tuesday night travel lectures
☐ Transfer facts to notebook

← (HOW.....Techniques)

Setting realistic target dates converts that stepping-up-to-be-off plan into your count-down chart. Remembering Henry Ford's advice that even the biggest challenges can be overcome when approached in small logical steps, all that remains is a formal declaration of war.

GLEANING INFORMATION

Wander-free existence is born of expedition readiness. Since limited knowledge can be expensive, knapsack travelers need a running start. With research, your travels officially begin.

Be selective. Book shelves and magazine racks bend under more material than you can use. Bibliographies provide clues to informational gems related to your interests. Review back issues of *Venture, Travel,* and *Holiday.* Your library carries almanacs, guides, or the New York telephone directory for addresses of government tourist offices. These, and airline tourist departments, supply mountainous free material, particulars on discounts, and personalized attention to specialized requests. Other sources include international business, cultural, and welfare organizations (e.g., Esso Touring Service, East-West Center, Asia Society, Pan American Union, UNESCO, International YMCA), museums of art and natural history, paperbacks (including novels), lectures, movies, and television specials. Pick the brains of returnees from abroad. A pocket-sized notebook is adequate repository for culled-down facts needed en route.

The moment you've had enough of other's theories, cool it. The important questions will be answered by experience.

Helpful Organizations

Globetrotters Club, B.C.M./Roving, London, W.C. 1, England
    Outstanding group for "how to get there for less than less." $2 per year brings *Globe* with articles on off-beat trips, columns for questions and traveling companions, and a hospitality service between far-flung members.

American Youth Hostels, 14 W. 8th St., New York, N.Y. 10011
    Information on hostel tours and inexpensive trans-Atlantic schedules. Listing of overseas youth hostels comes with membership, $7, or less for those under 20.

United States National Student Association (NSA), 265 Madison Ave., New York, N.Y. 10016
    Student travel publications, charter flights, International Student (discount) Card.

Council on Student Travel, 777 United Nations Plaza, New York, N.Y. 10016
    Student sailings, free literature on overseas programs and travel.

Helpful Publications

Material on visa requirements, health, customs, and passports
    Passport Office, Washington, D.C. 20524, free.

Current and reliable information on transportation along major travel routes, including local
    How to Travel Without Being Rich, by Norman Ford, Harian Publications, Greenlawn, L.I., N.Y. 11740, $1.50.

Maps

> National Geographic Society, 17th and M Sts., N.W., Washington, D.C. 20024 (Best overall maps; request list).
>
> Esso European Travel Aids, P.O. Box 142, Convent Station, N.J. 07961 (European countries, 25 cents each; Asian, African, Latin American maps locally available in each area).

Flight Information

> *Air Travel Bargains,* by Jim Woodman, Box 408, Coconut Grove, Miami, Fla. 33133, $2 (No surprises, but all the facts).

Freighter Information

> *Travel Routes Around the World,* by Frederic Tyarks and Norman Ford, Harian Publications, Greenlawn, L.I., N.Y. 11740, $1.00.
>
> *Sailing List* (monthly), Glaessel Shipping Corp., 44 Whitehall St., New York, N.Y. 10004, $2 yearly.

General Information

> *New Horizons,* $2 from Pan American Airways offices. (Revised yearly, concentrated information on 112 countries).

TRAVEL AGENTS

Finding a representative of the commercial travel industry who understands your financially subversive approach is rare, and usually unnecessary. Stateside agents can book departure transportation. You need no prearranged hotel, tour, or other local services. Overseas agents along your route are locally knowledgeable, and more affordable.

HOW MUCH ROUTE PLANNING?

When planning causes "cerebral indigestion," it's time to stop. Decide on certain high spots and crossroads to check out major transportation. Big hops can be arranged in advance by direct mail, or booked through an agent. Save some reading for in-between moments abroad. If, irretrievable days and miles later, you learn you've walked past an audience with the Living Goddess, it's time to dig a little deeper.

SLAYING DRAGONS

Don't let anyone discourage you on your plans. We're still batting close to a thousand on naive "can't do" and "you'll regret" advice from this side. The returning freelancer who expresses his regrets is an oddity we've never met. Three out of four blind approaches turn out well. The fourth becomes an adventure.

Dragons easily slain include: "It's too late to get bookings," "You'll never get a visa for...," "It's dangerous traveling in...," "But you can't speak the language," "You'll ruin your health," "They'll never let you into...," "You can't travel alone," "It's too expensive to...," "There are no hotels in...," "You can't travel in the rainy/dry/tourist season." Those dragons which can't be slain—"What about your job, future, savings, security?"—can be hoisted to the shelf to be handled on richer return.

GOING ON YOUR OWN

It's quite a trick trying to coordinate ground rules, dates, budget, and interests with another. You'll share experiences, reduce expenses, and keep each other hopping, but going alone provides your best insurance for seeing *all*. Hospitality extends more easily to an individual. The traveler's way is strewn with potential companions knowledgeable in the "we may pick up, rejoin, part as we desire with no hard feelings" code. A short tour can satisfy the starting-off desire for security.

CONSIDERING SEASONS

Let seasons influence, but not dictate, your itinerary. Countries in the tropics may place the choice between rainy and dry seasons. But the tourist "dry" season can be parched and dusty, and we've gone through extended "rainy" seasons comfortably cool without once unpacking raincoats. Most of the traveler's world is sufficiently varied to accommodate every climate concurrently. But don't ignore nature in planning ahead.

Off-season rates to, from, and in Europe are reduced. Departures before May 1 or after August 7, and returns before July 1 and after October 7 are considered "off-season" by sea; airlines vary more generously.

ARRANGING DOCUMENTS

Passport Get forms from nearest passport office, and return with proof of citizenship, identity, 2 photos, and $9.00 to passport office, federal or state court clerk.

Visas Certain intriguing countries insist on visitation approval rights through a clerical nuisance known as the visa. Their stamp is your croix de guerre for perseverance in travel's toughest battle. Get visas through 1) the agent selling your departure ticket, 2) mail, 3) visits to consulates in the United States, and 4) en route. The last gets you off sooner, but kills valuable time abroad, and may jeopardize visits to countries where political frictions exist. Visas are issued more graciously, and more frequently gratis, from consulates here. Tourist visas offer maximum privileges. Multiple-entry visas should be requested for hub countries such as India. Visa requirements can be obtained free when writing for your passport. Start early. A rotating paper clip on each visa page as required while traveling saves accordion confusion at ports of entry and exit.

V.I.P. Credentials Verification of student status (International Student Card, even an old bookstore identification) often entitles you to discounts (sometimes 50 per cent, *e.g.,* Turkey) on transportation, selective lodgings, and admissions. Taking a single extension course on where you're going can more than pay for itself through savings generated by your bursar's receipt. Getting an International Driver's License is a quick formality through AAA. YMCA membership brings discounts in "Y's" abroad. One African and a few Latin countries still insist on a fingerprinted police clearance. Character references on impressive letterheads, and a bank letter, sometimes satisfy visa requirements of countries usually looking for an on-going transportation ticket.

Health Certificate Shots are best endured from a "travelers' M.D." who has vaccines and the International Certificate (also available from airlines) on hand. (Smallpox revaccination is standard. Check *Health Hints for Travelers,* a pamphlet supplied by the passport office, when you get your passport for other inoculations possibly needed. Stapling the health certificate to the back inside page of your passport facilitates checking and prevents loss.

COPING WITH LANGUAGES

You'll get by with English, but any language skills you develop make for easier going. Pocket-sized phrase books as used by the Armed Forces (Price list #19—Superintendent of Documents, Washington, D.C. 20402) start at $.25. *Lyall's Guide to 25 Languages of Europe* is now available through Stackpole, $3.95.

Longer stays warrant some preparation with records. The World Publishing Company, Cleveland, Ohio 44102, has albums of 5-6 records each ($2.45) of helpful words and phrases in 30 languages. Others, including the "Living Language" series, are at your library.

DECIDING ON CURRENCIES

Carry funds in U.S. bills in money belts (see Chapter 3 for list "Clothing to Wear"), foreign currencies (see Chapter 8 on free and black markets), having at least enough to get you settled on arrival, or letter of credit or travelers' checks. If you use the latter, get lots of $20's and $10's for slower spending and less paper at points of exit.

Extreme fluctuations in currency values are becoming limited to fewer countries. Travelers with hard dollars can, however, still trade to advantage throughout a primarily soft-money world. Free markets exist in the U.S., for prior fueling, also in Europe, Tangier, Beirut, Aden, Singapore, Hong Kong. Black markets in local currency are found wherever official exchange rates have lost touch with reality.

BLUEPRINTING THE GREEN

Being strapped for funds prevents buckling up. From drawing board to launching may require, of some, an additional process called "blueprinting the green," subject: propellent. If your plans are funded, skip on to Chapter 3.

Squirreling Away   The game of saving is waged against the pressures of conformity on the playing field of a consumer economy. Your drive is towards the acquisition of experiences, not goods. The cost of an automobile can support you two or three years abroad. Your savings goal, therefore, isn't difficult, just different.

You can't squirrel away and still keep up with the Joneses. But the Joneses don't usually manage a winter in Zermatt, or the Taj Mahal by moonlight. To hear the great symphony orchestras in their native locale means holding back on the stereo and records for later.

The values of saving are known by most. Converting understanding to consistent practice leaves many behind. Keep your goals handy, for support. Stay tuned to your own drummer. A change of pace which stresses essentials builds more than the travel kitty. It brings you closer to the way you'll operate overseas. Adjustments now pave the way for extended travel and savings abroad.

Convert your income and expenditures to a business basis, using controls exercised by any prudent concern. Keep records. Justify purchases. Make use of incentives. Reinforce appropriate behavior. Keep a chart that pinpoints your special problems. Keep another on which you plot your upward progress.

Identifying Drains   Start a list of expenditures under such categories as food, transportation, purchases, gifts, entertainment. Let nothing escape recording. Tabulate at regular intervals; weekly, monthly, or the end of each pay period. Also keep an overall record for comparison checks. This identifies major escape routes of elusive dollars. Having spotted the drains, stem their flow.

Cutting Costs   Distinguish between essentials and non-essentials. Determine exactly how much might be saved at the beginning of each period. Put this in the bank untouched. Live on the remainder.

Get onto a cash basis. Charge accounts and credit cards make non-essential purchases all too easy, and add up to as much as 21 per cent in additional interest. Close the checking account, saving on its monthly costs and those casually written checks. Money orders serve as well when needed.

Shop scientifically. Stick to a prewritten list. Notice items prior to need, so that final purchase is on the basis of comparative values. Shop specials. Stay with the middle-price lines.

Food expenses high? You'll be doing a lot of eating out shortly, and can afford to save the French restaurants for France. Buy cheaper varieties and in quantity. Load up on "loss leaders" and in-season produce. Food coupon clippers can squirrel away another $1 to $1.50 a week. For the really eager there are low-priced foods, like MPF (Multi-Purpose Food).

Consider divorce proceedings if you're married to a car. If the roof above is a burdensome expense, weigh the merits of a move. Do you really need a phone? Cigarettes? The savings from one year's abstinence bought our friend's round-trip tickets to England.

Incentives, Devices, Compensations, and Pitfalls   All of these suggestions taken at once might result in a too-wrenching readjustment. As the former balance of life is disturbed, there must be adequate, if temporary, compensations and reinforcements. Your crash year of preparation is in no way going to be a normal one. Remind yourself that this reduced way of life is still enviable luxury by the standards of most you'll encounter abroad.

Post your objectives where they can serve as a daily reminder that this is for real. A sprinkling of travel posters may keep alive the message. Each time you've proudly accomplished your periodic saving goal, and the "company chart" sweeps into an upward curve, reward yourself. See a travel movie.

Start a cookie jar for all loose change, rebates, gifts, and "found" money. Every time you achieve a conscious saving by deciding against a cab, washing your own nylon shirts, or making up a week's lunches, immediately reward yourself by dropping in the saved amount. By themselves insignificant, taken together they'll take you around the world.

Let these accumulations earn interest with your regular savings. If you run short, borrow from yourself at a usurious rate of interest. "Vacation Club" accounts encourage regular contributions, but pay no interest. Accumulated interest in your own "See It Now" account adds another week or two to your time abroad at withdrawal.

Figure even the smallest saving on an annual, or overseas basis. When you turn down a cab, see it translated. It's an all-day bus trip in the Andes, or north to Kashmir. It's an extra day of meals and lodging in India. Introducing regularity to new money-saving routines will make them automatic.

Credit plans and bank loans will get you off, but not the hook. Unless this is your only time for travel, lures to "Go now, pay later" threaten high resolve and bright new plans upon return. Credit cards might extend a trip, but charge 1 per cent monthly on your bill's unpaid balance, and are limited to more expensive places outside the local economies.

Increasing your income through moonlighting is no substitute for squirreling away, which accomplishes the same result on your present income, with time to be human. But if these devices don't add up to a proper kitty, start in on that spare-time activity or part-time job.

Keep outlets from conflicting with ends. Pitfalls lie before the best laid plans. When you just have to cut loose, analyze your needs. Then modify the splurge so they are satisfied without jeopardizing the goals. Make it a paperback or the premium beer, not a new sports car.

WORKING YOUR WAY

Working your way is more romantic in sound than in practice. Like joining the Navy to see the world, there are easier ways. The work-away foregoes that experience of perfect freedom which can be now, and perhaps never again. Why limit yourself in advance? There's more room in a plan of "Work Hard, Play Hard" than "Pay as You Go."

Working your way cuts sightseeing and limits opportunities for meeting a broad range of people. It puts you back to what you've left — a routine. It holds you to those places which present no language problems, and where there's work, which are most like home. Chances of getting work suited to your talents and interests are slim. Even when there's no labor surplus, work permits are difficult to obtain. Salaries overseas are far from comparable, savings opportunities even less.

Worthwhile overseas jobs are landed through stateside procedures, for specific skills and contract periods, or through personal contacts. Casual jobs for the amateur arise mostly through strokes of luck.

If you simply must go now, working your way takes spirit, a liking for people, and the resiliency of a boxer who keeps getting back up off the mat. Write to the labor offices of selected countries, and read how others have done it in books like *Around the World on $80* by Robert Christopher (Holt, Rinehart and Winston), and *Around the World on $50*, by Joseph Bormel (Meador Publishing Co.).

There are ways your travels might be subsidized. Ads in the personals columns of the *Saturday Review* and large dailies list occasional opportunities. You can serve as a part-time business representative for small U.S. firms; spot items for import firms or collectors; be a children's nurse, companion, English instructor; take commercially useful photographs; write for overseas English newspapers or U.S. periodicals; and on a unique venture (not usually your first), find product sponsors.

More typically, the ease and low costs of knapsackery should make working unnecessary.

CHAPTER 3

SELECTING KNAPSACK, BUCKLING UP

A proper bindle, plus what you've gathered, divided by three, modified by weight requirements and rounded off to essentials in harmonious balance, equals traveling light and with a smile. Snapsackery is not for the over-sacksed.

Select an undisturbed corner as your staging area. What to stow then becomes a relaxed sorting process that's one part anticipation, two parts subtraction. Original designs for gracious living undergo revision with the gradual reduction of traditional items to those you really need. Or, start with basic living essentials and build up your kit. NASA has proved it can be done.

SELECTING KNAPSACK

Pick a pack that's sturdy and light. It will have to travel with the rest of you—all of you—comfortably.

Frameless knapsacks save a few pounds on weight, and are cheaper initially. But they're hard lugging, and contours depend on the stuffing. Frame packs retain their shape, balance easier, let air circulate between you and the load, and keep hard items from rubbing your back. Pack boards and newly popular independent pack frames carry heavier loads, but are better suited to trail camping. Projecting rigging is easily bent or broken by the demands of travel.

Look for a knapsack with a built-in metal carrying frame. European alpine-type knapsacks (rucksacks) are well-adapted to overseas travel. With the supporting frame a structural part, for cushioning and ventilation, your pack has no projections. It keeps its shape, regardless of load, and has several handy outside pockets.

Our Bergans packs have stood up well. Made in Norway, they're available from Abercrombie and Fitch, Madison Avenue and 45th St.,

New York, N.Y. 10017, for $31. Camp and Trail Outfitters, 112 Chambers Street, New York, N.Y. 10007 carry the C & T frame rucksack #316 (20 1/2" x 24" x 8") with three outside pockets, for $26.95. Surplus outlets occasionally have used U.S. Army frame packs, modeled on the Bergans, for around $9.95.

Base your final choice of this lifetime traveling companion on quality. Check for light frame, closely woven waterproof material, top-quality leather, double stitching, reinforced corners and edges, expandibility, and pockets. Also pick up sleeping bag extension straps ($1.75, from Abercrombie and Fitch) and cushioning pads for the shoulder straps ($2.50, A & F). Tump lines and waist belts are strictly trail items.

Ladies wishing to avoid an Atlas complex can select a slightly smaller pack. Camp and Trail's #316A (19" x 22" x 7") sells for $25.95. Abercrombie and Fitch's ladies' Bergans is $29.

An optional second bag for daily use and side trips completes the outfit. Canvas shoulder type is easiest to carry, but airlines bags collapse to fold away when not desired. Either can be your steady when there's a chance to drop off Big Brother. The Orvis Company, Manchester, Vt. 05254 has a tan fabric sportsman's bag (16" x 12" x 4") with adjustable carrying strap, for $5.75. L. L. Bean's, Freeport, Me. 04032 has a heavy-duty haversack (14" x 12" x 5") of duck and leather which features zippered envelope pocket and 2" strap, for $9.90. Abercrombie and Fitch carry a compact (14" x 10" x 4") English haversack for $7.00.

...AND ACCOMPANYING COSTUME

Multipurpose clothing and quick-drying washables serve the space-age knapsack traveler's major needs for staying light. In picking what to pack, stick with top-quality lines and comfortable styles.

Your basic outfit is what you wear at takeoff. Officer cadets, faced with daily clothing inspections, have proved that a single set of underwear and socks, washed nightly, serves through six months of training. You might prefer a less spartan "one on, one clean, one in the wash" approach. Clothing replacement en route is cheaper and more fun than lugging from home. This list covered a seven-month trip we took.

Clothing to Wear

His	Hers
Sturdy, all-purpose (i.e., acceptable in polite company) walking shoes	Same (broken-in)
Thick comfortable socks	Same, when wearing
Quick-drying nylon shorts and "T" shirt	Similar, plus half-slip
Washable trousers, held up with leather money belt (zipper lining in back)	Dark dacron-cotton wrap-around skirt with pockets
Drip-dry shirt	Drip-dry blouse with roll-up sleeves
Light washable zipper windbreaker with pockets	Same, feminine styling, with kerchief in pocket
Watch	

Clothing in Knapsack

His	Hers
Spare socks, shorts, "T" shirt	Additional socks, panties, bra
Heavy sweater	Same, just smaller
Light, crease-resistant sports jacket	Two dresses: one dacron, dressy; one seersucker shirtwaist with roll-up sleeves
White dacron polyester dress shirt, dacron tie, tieclasp	
Cotton-dacron sports shirt	Cotton-dacron sleeveless blouse
Non-wrinkle trousers	Dacron pleated skirt
	Slacks, for mountains only
Swim trunks	Swim suit, cap
Plastic raincoat (pocket size)	Plastic raincoat, rainkerchief
	Sneakers
	Pajamas

That's it, and it sufficed for a presidential audience, breakfast with royalty, after-hours spots, and Vienna's opera. In colder climates add a layer or two of underthings. On mountain trips rent, borrow, or buy, then mail home, that Kurd cap, pair of bearskin gloves, or Afghan sheeplined jacket.

Woman Talk: Don't be dependent on slow, rock-pounded laundry services or new adventures in dry cleaning. Nylon is easiest to handle, but drip-dry materials of part or 100 per cent cotton are more comfortable than non-absorbent synthetics in the tropics, and they dry sufficiently fast. Ventilating fabrics include seersucker, cotton knits, and cotton-dacron combos. Dacron "creampuff" stays crisp, is fairly cool, and good for the one dress-up outfit. Permanently pleated or gored skirts are comfortable, versatile, and pack as well as straight skirts.

Man Talk: Have one change to dignity; jacket or suit. A beard adds days to a trip. Get past the scraggly fungus stage and you too can be taken for Che Guevara or the Second Coming. A beard also makes you look 1) tough, and/or 2) wise, and/or 3) more attractive to the ladies. It doesn't itch. You save on time and blades. But don't be taken in by a radically changed self-image.

SPECIAL EQUIPMENT

Each of us carried a 2 1/2-pound down-filled "mummy" sleeping bag. We divided the remaining items between our two knapsacks as follows: a large plastic sheet; plastic quart bottle; toilet articles (break up a bulky kit; cosmetics, small towel, soap, toothbrushes, toothpaste); sunglasses; extra laces; rechargeable flashlight; small transistor radio; camera, film; paperbacks, maps, condensed notes; documents, extra photos; vitamins, prescription and tummy drugs, Empirin, band-aids; detergent powder, inflatable hangers, stretch clothesline; tissues, toilet paper, tampons, Wash 'n Dris; sewing kit, safety pins; small cooking pot, utensils set, can opener, emergency rations; insect stick repellent, snakebite kit, teargas pen; matches; and extra plastic bags. Regular campers might add the versatile Army surplus poncho, mosquito head net, additional first aid and eating supplies.

Forget stationery. Airletters are everywhere, and cheaper. Shoeshines come under the jurisdiction of free hotel services and numerous small boys. Instead of lugging guide books, take the important few ounces of detached pages, or distilled notes. Have a few paperbacks, but since these are available in capital cities, select only those for immediate or treasured reading. Toilet paper is best carried off the roll, in tightly wound wads, with a small (frequently replenished) supply in your pocket. Refill anything from glass into plastic bottles. When going by air don't fill any bottle to the top, and place it in a leak-proof bag. Take an all-purpose vitamin. Tropical travelers might carry salt tablets, but it's easier to just sprinkle every meal with additional salt.

Experienced trail packers will have more than usual knapsack space. Unlike camping preparedness, which calls for self-sufficiency, you'll find food wherever there are people.

Photography is best limited to one camera—the finest you can afford —and, except for filter and sun shade, forget the gadgets. You can do better on camera purchase abroad. Knapsackers starting off with a new camera should develop manipulative facility and allow for learner's mistakes before leaving. Kodachrome is scarce in some countries, but can be replenished in all free ports. Film wrapped in "Tropic Packs" costs no extra, or you can remove cylinders of film from regular packs, tighten or tape the lids, then fit cylinders compactly into a double plastic bag containing silica gel.

A transistor radio won't give you up-to-date information on such things as revolutions, but will convey the flavor of a place and keep you posted on the monosyllabic Voice of America slant on things. Tiny "travelers' packages" of impotent soap are better left for the real thing, securely wrapped in double plastic bags. A net bag takes little space but may emerge to carry temporary extras. Don't push your knapsack's expandibility to the limits. Leave room for overseas accumulations.

GIFTS AND TRADE GOODS

Small gifts say more than "thank you" to someone who's helped you along your way. Ingenious traders also manage to subsidize their travels by importing reasonable quantities of locally scarce personal goods for distribution in non-industrial countries. Gifts and goods needn't all be hauled from home. Duty-free shops at ports of exit, or free ports en route, invite bargain purchases as well as personal restocking.

Premium items vary with country and times. Likely to continue popular in major blocs of the world are: Kennedy half-dollars, U.S. jazz records, unusual flower seeds, nylon shirts and stockings, instant coffee, transistorized equipment, watches, cameras, liquor, lipsticks, ballpoint pens, and photos of yourself and family.

FINAL PACKING CEREMONY

You're ready to fit together a jigsaw puzzle which probably still has too many pieces. Keep like items together. Rolling or folding each article of clothing in a plastic bag helps prevent wrinkling and soiling. Small items go into the corners of larger. Practice-pack until it's right. There's a best place for every item. Once you've decided where that is, with rearrangements as experience suggests, keep it there.

Final packing order is a tight-rope act between competing factors:

1) *Distribution of weight*   The knapsack is carried more comfortably when heavier items are packed forward and towards the top, distributing weight across the shoulder blades. Sleeping bag might join heavy sweater and clothing as light bulk for the bottom, unless you use it nightly and thus prefer it buckled under the top flap.

2) *Accessibility*   Frequently used items are more accessible from the top, so stack in reverse priority order. Items of ready call belong in the outer pockets.

3) *Protection*   Easily damaged or fragile items go near the middle or bottom, well wrapped against pressure and movement. Projections and attachments invite tearing and loss.

Your knapsack, weighing around 30 pounds, should be comfortable on the shoulders, snug against the back. Try it out. A staggering first hoist by unused muscles needn't alarm, since a few days of carrying make for easy-swinging your way. If you find yourself leaning strongly forward, better repack. Balanced you can go all day, not that you'll have to. Slated for the side bag are passport, tickets, notebooks, pocket-slim phrase books, money, camera, film, and anything else to be kept close by.

STAYING LIGHT

To keep from becoming a sad sack-dragging pack rat, maintain replaceable expendibles at a minimum. Ship back, or give away, items no longer needed, marking packages "Personal effects, U.S. purchased." Periodic accumulations of books go cheaper via book rate. Films for processing are best sent home in prepurchased mailers, and left to await your arrival. Recipients can be alerted on correctable defects. Entrust purchases and gifts to reliable mails for duty-free (if under $10) and backpacking advantages. If the final load seems less than ordinarily dragged on a three-day weekend, you're set.

DEPARTURE CHECKLIST

☐ Overseas contact addresses set (Care of U.S. Consulate is reliable)

☐ Knapsack identified with tag which gives home address and refers possible finder to nearest U.S. consulate

☐ Passport number memorized; travelers' check numbers, inoculation dates, prescriptions, etc., recorded separately

☐ Medical.and dental check-out complete

☐ Initial currency exchange needs met

☐ Twenty-five single dollar bills packed

☐ Spare emergency bill secreted in safe place

☐ Baggage insurance considered

☐ Post Office, phone, newspaper, utilities, and hard-breathing draft boards notified

CHAPTER 4

FACTS ON BUDGET TRANSPORTATION

Being independent and flexible doesn't mean going blindly. The knapsack way suggests developing an acquaintance with in-transit and local possibilities. Then book the big hops for departure, and perhaps return.

Transportation is a knapsacker's biggest expense, but time and patience are excellent substitutes for money. When using both sea and air, it's usually best to go slowly, return quickly. Except for selected passages by sea, the necessity for advanced bookings is greatly exaggerated. But check. Onward arrangements to the Middle East, Africa, and Asia are accomplished more easily, less expensively from Europe. Local carriers charge fares geared to their economy. International carriers, while sometimes more reliable, may charge up to twenty times the local tariff.

The slower your means of transport, the less expensive it usually becomes—and the more interesting. The closer you get to an area, the easier it is to obtain accurate information about it, and the more mythical difficulties begin to fade. A broad sampling of all the available kinds of transport adds, like nothing else, to the spice of travel.

STRETCHING TIME

Most transoceanic passenger traffic now moves by air, with last-minute bookings rarely a problem. Not all airlines charge the same fare. Members of the International Air Transport Association (IATA) have fixed rates usually higher than reliable independent and local airlines. Bargain flights generally await your arrival on foreign shores. Setting off, however, Icelandic Airlines, a non-IATA carrier, has reduced fares to Europe. Flying lowest fares to Latin America are TAN and APSA Peruvian Airlines. There is, at this writing, no reduced flight over the Pacific, but the market may bring a revival of service.

41

One advantage of IATA lines is their commitment to cover expenses in delays and some reroutings. Often you must ask. Intra-European airfares of even IATA carriers are cheaper when booked abroad, less yet on night tourist flights. Additional discounts are available with International Student Identity Cards. A short vacation traveler should book round-trip to the farthest destination, visiting nearer cities on a free stopover basis.

Typical charter fares run New York to Tokyo, $520 roundtrip; Washington to Geneva, $200 roundtrip. Organized a group (usually 15) and your fare is free. Occasionally you can unearth an agent authorized to book you, at charter rates, on the scheduled flights of a new, less-traveled IATA carrier. The advantage is flexible date of return. There are unannounced special flights to be flushed out, such as a West Indies immigrant flight from Barbados to London via New York, for $200. Also consider points of embarkation. APSA's fare, New York to Bogotá, is $254; from Miami, it's $150.

Some purists insist, once abroad, that flying is for softies. The only alternative, over abundant stretches, is to bushwack or paddle. Besides keeping or picking up on a schedule, air travel deposits you with more energy. Meals are "free," worth two on the ground— three, when you stash rolls, cheese, and fruit into the "barf bag" for breakfast. When covering areas sticky about visas, an air ticket can save days of bureaucratic delay.

Some stretches are actually cheaper by air. Least expensive freighters to Panama charge $120 (from eastern ports). Via loosely interconnecting busses add at least two weeks of food and lodging to fares approximating $65 (from southern border towns). The flight from Miami totals $58. Another $50 leaves you in the high Andes of Ecuador. New York to the West Indies comes to $45 (on TransCaribbean Flight 101), exactly one-third the lowest fare by sea. You can fly from San Francisco to Hawaii, Japan, Taiwan, Hong Kong, the Philippines, South Vietnam, Cambodia, Malaysia, Indonesia, Thailand, Burma and Calcutta, with a year's stopover privileges, for $634. This combination, using individually booked ships, would cost considerably more and could take a year. From Calcutta westward to the Atlantic, advantages clearly lie with surface transportation.

STRETCHING MONEY

Going by sea is still the most popular way to collect yourself, and can start a single traveler's chain of onward adventures through new-found friends. Stateside passenger bookings are increasingly expensive, with limited "tourist" accommodations snapped up early. Passenger fares also never include total costs, though you can hold these in line.

Opportunities for stretching funds by sea remain, however, on certain cargo lines, tramp steamers (available at short notice), and off-season liners. Beyond the trans-Atlantic run, ships from overseas ports are often thinly booked, with foreign companies usually cheaper than American.

Days of transoceanic steerage are past. But cans of happy programmed sardines, known as "student ships," arranged by AYH, NSA, and CST (addresses in chapter 2), transport thousands annually.

Freighters aren't always the cheapest way to go. Despite 2-cent cokes and nickel beers, passenger luxuries are increasingly reflected in rising fares. U.S. cargo ships are the most up-to-date, fastest, and reliable for departure, also the most expensive. Up-to-date freighter guides identify the better bargains. But cheapest onward fares booked from abroad (e.g., Ceylon to Japan, $70) go unlisted. Let comparison shopping for a freighter take you up the gangplanks as well as to the harbor master and commercial houses with their chalked boards of departures. Port city newspapers list arrivals and departures.

Best hunting for European-bound freighters is in less populated eastern ports—Baltimore, Norfolk, Canada's Quebec and St. John. Hugo Stinnes Lines has cabins for $125 one way from Norfolk. Head and Lord Line fares start at $130. Tramp steamers are joined through a chat with the captain, who must be convinced you can adapt.

Working your way is limited to Scandinavian and small Japanese lines, and occasional freighters under lesser-known flags, who hire men as deckhands and messboys, girls as stewardesses.

Through Interchange, you can plan an extensive sea-air itinerary with round-trip deduction on circuits. As departure draws near, attempts to coordinate dates, however, often end with a hastily written air ticket. Even when successfully underway, vagaries of steamship schedules can throw you off, while passengers whose freighters actually connect often report disappointment with rigid schedules. When your plan is a combination of air, sea, and overland, decide at the outset to be responsible for your own pacing and arrangements.

DEALS ON WHEELS

The beauty of knapsack travel is the independence it affords. When, through purchase, you commit yourself to a specific combination of wheels, you'll go mostly where they can take you. Hike over a mountain and continue through villages on the other side? Not likely. Meet people? Not as freely as when using public conveyances. You spend more time riding, and a good part of your travel fund is tied up in the apparatus.

Customs regulations have reduced advantages in ordering a vehicle abroad. Add unsung pitfalls of paperwork, border tape, foreign driving habits, gas prices, hours of roadwork, and the gamble of sale at destination versus shipping costs, and you might prefer being hitched only to a knapsack.

Motor bike, scooter? Great in Europe, and easily carried on trains, they're a problem on poor roads beyond. Accident rates are high, carrier packs easily pilfered. You're dependent on climate, and could wind up more of a loner than you'd like to be.

An expedition approach, for easiest camping, requires wheels. Our Volkswagen convertible's seats recline into beds. Camper wagons, camper units for pick-ups ($500 to $1000, or build-it-yourself for $100), telescoping tent trailers, and retired hearses guarantee reservations. But why carry a bucket where you can stop at any fountain? Public transportation overseas is so much cheaper, and often more efficient than here at home.

When you really need wheels, rent. Local agencies, always cheaper, often rent the same car for half or less the fees of international organizations. For the price of a scooter you can travel *and* live a summer in Europe. The equivalent of your investment in a camper or car can take two people around the world.

BOUNCING ALONG

Transplanted from jet streams to knapsack means, a knapsacker's do-it-yourself circuit begins in earnest. Bouncing, puffing, and grinding along within a broad spectrum between hitchhiking and effortless jet, are 1057 flavorful varieties of local transportation.

You can continue to almost anywhere, booking as you go, by investigating onward transportation first thing on arrival at each new place. When delayed, take side trips, read, hitchhike, or skip aloft. Shrinking time forces a choice when some forms of transportation, by their slowness, prevent you from savoring all that's worthwhile at destination. Occasionally you might want to join others in renting a jeep or boat for special treks.

BUSSES AND REASONABLE FACSIMILES

Localest of local transport is the bus. Fares are nominal, capacities phenomenal. Your knapsack irreverently joins vegetables, fruits, flowers, heaped aloft. An overwhelmed ticket seller can be found near the center of a chattering group. Your cue on fare, seldom over a dollar, comes from transactions of fellow passengers who'll see you're not cheated.

Many of these hinterland projectiles are homemade structures built over a standard truck chassis. You are usually offered the seat of honor by the driver. From occasional Mercedes (Oriental hostesses serve iced towels, tea, and snacks) to rattletrap mammy wagons, you'll love the busses.

Several London groups operate long-haul budget coaches overland to India. Trips include camping and average two months.

TRAINS, TOY AND OTHERWISE

You'll marvel at plucky coal- and wood-burning puffing "billies," circle curves, switchbacks, miniature 19th-century carriages, and stops for animals on the tracks. Sit forward, facing rear, to be spared fallout. Pakistan has purdah cars for the ladies. A Peruvian coach may be lit by oil lamps, and when you cross the Andes' highest pass (15,693'), free oxygen comes with your ticket. First class in Ecuador consists of wooden benches and a john. Second class is with the same hard seats but no john. Third class offers movable benches in a boxcar. Fourth class passengers congregate without benches, and bumpy fifth class has the best view, but gets windy—on top.

Rail travel in Europe, any class, is a treat. European railways

(British, Swiss) offer thrift reductions on tickets when purchased in America. Eurail passes offer unlimited first-class western European travel. Lower-class rail is half or less the first-class fare. Going for less presents no problem in the industrialized nations, including Japan. Out beyond, a few new rules apply.

Third-class rail may test your love for humanity among, for example, the "untouchables" of India. But since India's middle class has grown faster than her number of second-class railway carriages, third class can be less crowded than second-class. And third-class reserved bunks cost less than second-class coach seats, where there's no assurance of sitting. Tickets for a three-day rail trip across northern India can be purchased for $4.14. Sophisticated travelers ride above, in the baggage racks, a definite promotion from passenger-at-large status in the melee below. This is common practice in Pakistan and Ceylon as well as India, where passengers carry their own bedrolls. If the train begins its run from your station, let a porter "reserve" an overhead perch by laying out your sleeping bag full length before the train rolls alongside the platform.

Check ahead on train times, asking several people to arrive at a consensus. Occasionally reservations are necessary in all classes. When this creates competition between money-waving hopefuls, standing aside with dignity usually brings the station master to your assistance.

When traveling without reservation by lower-class rail, get to the station well before departure to stake out a seat. Take along a good book. In a few spots, like Indonesia, locals with no intention of riding may claim space until the highest bidder takes over, sending them home with a coin.

If there's any question, the station master probably speaks English, or can find someone to help. Buy the lowest-priced ticket first. If too crowded, convert to the next class. Sweater or sleeping bag makes wooden benches more comfortable.

If lower-class rail is occasionally exhausting, remember, you're traveling for pennies. Sometimes it's your only door into the local peasantry's way of life.

BOATS, BARGES, AND BATHTUBS

The rivers of East Pakistan, Southeast Asia, and Brazil's extensive Amazon Valley have round-the-clock services a local peasant or knapsack peon can afford. Some of the world's most gorgeous scenery (Africa's Lake Victoria, Japan's Inland Sea) can be leisurely sailed for under a penny a mile. Other busy waters (the Mediterranean, off West Africa, the Caribbean) offer myriad possibilities for longer jaunts.

Caribbean island-hopping by regular passenger-cargo ship with meals and cabin averages $20 a day, less on longer trips. Knapsack toters might prefer carrying their own food and the more romantic alternative of climbing aboard a native sloop for roughly a dollar a day. A West Indies "Fix-It Mon" can put you atop an interisland barge or on the decks of a three-masted schooner. Yachting tourists frequently seek extra crew.

Elsewhere you can rent jungle dugouts or ride the mail boat. Fishing boats and coastal steamers are easy passage, but if they go up empty, so may your stomach. Deck passage is cheapest, and recommended for short hauls and balmy days.

Water provides your most economical form of transportation. While an Amazonian tourist agency charges $21 for three hours of back-country boating, scouting the local docks reveals a regular all-day native launch for 32 cents. Many skippers welcome passengers, particularly a foreigner. If it moves your way and floats, why not ask?

UNIDENTIFIED FLYING OBJECTS

Domestic flights, cheaper and more colorful than international, provide the best, if not only, access to large undeveloped pockets of terra firma. It's possible to find a nationally subsidized hop to a border town, picking up overland, or by air again, after making the crossing below. Air travel suffers when compared to wanderings amongst the grass roots of changing habitat and culture. But as long as flying depends on people, count on surprises.

Some domestic airlines handle meals by landing, then transporting passengers in land rover or dugout to the local boarding house. Back-country flight times are scheduled at "more or less," because the absence of beacons curtails traffic after dark.

Airport transfers can be a major drain. Don't be overwhelmed by the first rush of taxi pushers. Ask an employee about local busses. Some airlines provide free transport, as do certain hotels, but chances are you won't be staying in them. Airline microbusses, operating between town offices and airport, are primarily for their own personnel but often offer a ride. If you've met a local resident on the flight, the problem is probably solved before you've even landed. Frequently U.S. personnel, out to greet a visitor or friends, will offer a lift. Take your time, investigate, and your knapsack chances for a friendly informative ride are good.

Should a taxi be in order, try to share. Make sure, in the bustle of loading, that the meter doesn't start from where the last fare ended. If there are no meters, don't enter until briefed by a disinterested clerk. Establish the rate before you leave the curb.

If flying out again, leave extra gear with customs or the airline. Take just what's needed for the kind of stay planned.

OTHER ASSORTED AND SORDID MEANS

Local modes of basic transportation can provide some of your most fruitful experiences. You may go by elephant, but in the natural course of getting from one place to another—also by horse, donkey, mule, camel, and bullock cart—in lànd rover, jeep, bus, lorry, mammy wagon, and money bus—by narrow gauge, broad gauge, and three-mile-high train, tram, subway, steam engine, cable car, and cog railway—plane, from canvas-covered and prewar piston to jet—gondola, canoe, dugout, shikara, launch, barge, ferry, sailboat, fishing boat, government yacht, freighter, passenger liner, coastal steamer, hydrofoil, and side-wheeler—bike, motor scooter, motorcycle, sidecar, pedicab (alias trishaw, triped, or bicycle rickshaw), motorized rickshaw, tonga, go-kart, thumb, Kashmiri sled. Some are conveyances, others "conveyances." Try them. But fight back.

Hiking and biking assure knapsackers intimate contact with country-side and people. Cycles are easily purchased and resold. From Kano to Katmandu, you can also rent. Bag's too large? Send heavier things ahead. Or pack up the extras and seamail them home. Save cycling for compact, scenic spots, where your goal is depth.

Shank's mare and knapsack still identify the most independent of all travelers. Favorite haunts for pedijaunts include the Alps, Himalayan foothills, Wordsworth's lakes, the Japanese countryside. Distances and time become incidental when, as in the Black Forest, there are routes and trails to suit any mood. Or trek the secluded bays of a tropical island, such as easily reached St. John in the Virgins. Let supper be served from late afternoon spear-gun shopping in an underwater supermarket, with a new beach each night. Or take the toy train to Darjeeling, where Everest-experienced Sherpas, using British-built Dak bungalows as way stations, will, for 75 cents a day, lead you to the edge of the world's roof.

HITCHHIKERY

This word on thumb fun is for those inclined, and those whose fortunes have declined. Most will prefer the reliability of inexpensive public transportation. There will be times, however, when waving the wand of the upturned thumb can help you make transportation connections as well as open a culture's hidden doors.

Apply your judgment to each changing set of circumstances. Hitchhiking can be recommended in more areas than even the most dedicated thumber can ever cover. It's perfectly acceptable for girls to hitchhike in Europe and other Continental outposts. We'd advise the team approach, and no less than the normal precautions. Traveling couples seem to inspire the greatest confidence.

Where Hitchhiking Is Easiest   Territories endowed with a sense of stability, where trust is a common commodity (Britain, Holland, Scandinavia, Australia) make for easier thumbing. Our free-wheeling export also enjoys acceptance where individuality is encouraged, the zestful spirit respected (former British colonies, including eastern and southern Africa, Canada, Australia, New Zeland; Germany and Austria for "autoschtopping"; and Israel, where it's getting a "tramp"

Also inviting to the global hitchhiker are areas where regular transport is poor, or where curiosity and compassion play a role (Southern Europe, Africa, the Middle East). Europe's traffic makes for more frequent rides. Wide open spaces elsewhere make for longer waits, but longer lifts.

Where transportation is scarce, drivers may seek payment. Clear the arrangements at outset. In Israel there's hitchhiking on any army vehicle going your way, by law. France has announced a hitchhiking card, including insurance benefits. Poland's hitchhiking insurance is government-subsidized.

Enticing a Lift   Before getting on any highway, first check around town. What's the traffic pattern to where you're going? Let it be known at the central hotel that you can spell off on driving.

Approaching a traveler about to check in after a day behind the wheel, one young man might offer, with few rejections, to continue onward while the owner slept. Daylight is preferable for many reasons, but another good after-sundown source is truck drivers.

Appearance, being neatly dressed to the purpose, is vital to getting rides. In some countries it pays to look foreign, i.e., American. Mobility deteriorates with appearance. Stand in front of the knapsack. Shoulder bag goes sneakily behind. Smoking, conversation with a companion, or less than full attention to an oncoming potential host divides both his attention and feelings about you. The most effective aspect of appearance is a smile, which spells "pleasant company."

Finding the best place to start may call for a hike, bus, or tram to the edge of town, where traffic has filtered to what's going your way. At a well-worn spot beyond the first road sign is your launching pad. Drivers must slow down to confirm their bearings. You can be seen, checked over, and identified with a particular destination. Beyond that, any place with visibility, a cause for slowing traffic, and room for a safe turnoff is good.

When another aspirant is entrenched, courtesy suggests a cheerful greeting and taking up not quite out of sight beyond. After your temporary rival has been snatched off, you're free to move to center stage. You may be invited to join the ride. If more hitches await the end of this lift, "three's a crowd." Independent thumbers, with the possible exception of couples, travel faster. When there are more than two in your crowd, split up after picking a rendezvous spot for the night. Correctly judging traffic, sizing up a potential host, and accepting the kind of ride suited to your needs, can send you sailing past your predecessor.

Wait for what appears to be a long ride. A dozen short hops can't beat one to the door unless you desire that broad a sampling of the local folks. Walking while hitchhiking cuts your chances for a lift. Better to hike to a good spot and then stay primed for a ride from there.

Map familiarity makes it easier to politely decline any offer that could leave you isolated from onward traffic or lodging. Using a road map, get out well before your driver has turned off into nowhere.

Hitchhikers have used gimmicks designed to draw a passing motorist's eye, or sympathy. No device can compete with the assurance of pleasant company from a genuine smile, beamed straight at the driver.

Requests for a lift are not always made by thumb. Some local gestures resemble scratching an itchy palm, holding off a muddy pup, pushing back an incoming tide, or undulating one hand like an upside-down jelly fish. Just standing with knapsack usually carries the message.

What about signs? Perhaps it depends on how far your destination, or how charmingly it's misspelled in the local language. Be sure the friendly man in the last town hasn't written out something for you which reads, "To hell with the National Party," although in some spots that would really get you rides. Foreign knapsackers like to sew their country's flag to the pack. You can pin yours for easy detachment.

Early birds get the long hop. Drivers out to cover long distances start with the sun, in hot countries before dawn. Stay off side roads if you wish to make time. This is no problem in half the world, where there's just one road in your direction. Don't let a longer lift tempt you past intended stopovers.

Peace Corps, USIS, AID, consular services, and American construction companies in less-developed areas have regular runs for mail, supplies, and personnel on leave. Drivers between projects and major population centers are usually delighted to offer an empty seat and a few onward tips as well. Of course, anyone who parasitically starts relying on U.S. personnel overseas is in for the grand cold shoulder.

Rules of the Road   Once aboard and rolling, the introductions made, you may choose not to mention your more distant destination until assessment of driving habits and mutual compatibility. Let the driver lead, giving him a chance to become comfortable with you. From this point on, you're prepared to do more than your share, which could be anything from sitting on contraband to feeding the oxen. You'll wish to become neither a burden nor extra expense. This may require conversing only as he seems to desire it, which may be extensively, even though you speak different languages, and smoking only after requesting permission.

Besides reciprocating your host's generosity through the quality of your company, you may find other opportunities at meal and rest stops. Chances are, unless you're defending U.S. foreign policy from the first closing slam of the door, your time together will go all too quickly. You'll learn about another area and its activities from the rarely penetrated local frame of reference, and from confidences shared by people who never expect to see you again. Conclude your conversation

51

and thanks, exchanging addresses if inclined, prior to drop point, for a speedy exit creating no traffic problems.

Quite often your driver, rejuvenated by your efforts to reach his own backyard, develops an interest in usually ignored, if world-famous, sights. It's only fair to share the costs of more extensive touring. Frequently you'll receive invitations home. It takes no sixth sense to judge if the invitation is straightforward.

Precautions   When surly, off-color, or alcoholic comments provide tipoffs to possible trouble, have your tactful refusal ready. Some advise girls to carry a hatpin. Finding a traveling companion seems more sound. If you find your ride a problem, use some ready-made excuse for getting off. Should you anticipate resistance, don't reveal alarm, but be ready to open the door with one hand, grabbing bag in the other at the next slowdown of traffic, particularly where there are people on the street. Regular hitchhikers should not carry all their money in cash.

HITCHHIKING BY SEA AND AIR

Occasionally the power of the upturned thumb extends beyond the lorries and limousines of the open road to the air and high seas. It usually takes one or more of the following:

1) *Sleuthing*   Little-known provisions, loopholes, exceptional procedures for obtaining conventional transport, including knowing when to be where, cannot be broadcast, but are gained from getting to know someone in the business. Civil Service employees, for example, are permitted free hops on Coast Guard flights, including destinations like Madrid and Saigon.

2) *Boldness*   Travel agents, airline employees, reservists, members of a maritime union, enjoy special travel privileges. Making the contacts and acquiring quasi-legal credentials is for the extremely bold.

3) *Charm*   Captains of tramp steamers are permitted passenger leeway not so easily granted by larger companies. Think of all the reasons a skipper might want you as his personal guest. Such arrangements are easier in West African, West Indies, and Pacific ports, and on coastal freighters, fishing boats, interisland schooners, and river craft.

With conventional formalities ignored in politically unsettled areas, military and private contract aircraft of freelance companies have been known to fly budget travelers in the Congo, Vietnam, and Laos, no questions asked. Airlifts which go one way empty, shuttle planes into U.S.-supported areas of Southeast Asia, small airlines under U.N. contract, cargo flights on special assignments—these are your tramp steamers of the air. The more remote the spot, the better your chances for a brotherly lift.

4) *Destitution*   What's sometimes called hitchhiking is, more accurately, a work-away agreement arranged by a relief organization to get Penniless Percival off their hands.

If your travel plans absolutely depend on this fortuitous extension of the traditional powers of the thumb, you'll likely run into serious disappointment.

CHAPTER 5

BUDGET-MINDED ACCOMMODATIONS

Many a happily sailing traveler has been blown off course by the hotel bill. Knapsackers insist on a broad definition of the word "Hotel." Accommodations, not an end but a means, are to lay one's head, fill up, stretch out, and anything else in order to travel. Somewhere between a haystack and the Royal Suite, there'll always be shelter available.

BUDGET PRINCIPLES

The following may ease the trial-and-error process of getting nested without mortgaging onward aspirations.

1) An inexpensive place is the one in which to explore, rest, recreate. When reaching an expensive spot, go like the wind. Don't by-pass the cities. But save relaxation for the next economy inn, soaking up the local scene while comfortably preparing for the next pit of pole-vaulting onward. Capital cities are reputedly expensive. Keen explorers find the opposite can also be true.

2) Less-touristed hotels needn't be uncomfortable. But, shave your standards on comfort a bit, and you'll save more than 50 per cent of your total budget. "To be a good traveler", says Tuckerman, "a sweet landscape must sometimes atone for an indifferent supper, and an interesting ruin charm away the remembrance of a hard bed". At worst, you'll occasionally sleep on sheet-covered rope beds or hammocks in the tropics, and wash from tanks of rain water.

3) Increase your adaptability by carrying a small lightweight sleeping bag. It serves as a cozy envelope against chill weather and rump softener when sardined against the rock-and-roll sides of a train or bus. The sheet sleeping sack, frequently required for admission to youth hostels, can be used on top of bedding in marginal caravansaries. A

compact plastic sheet can be placed between occasionally questionable mattresses and sleeping bags. Weighing a few ounces, it also serves as a tent for outdoor overnights.

4) Let neither false pride nor pressures from others push you into an accommodation beyond your needs. Take less experienced companions, familiar only with conventional hotels, exploring for that side-street inn.

Locals, who'd like you to form the best impression of their country, will, if you let them, establish you in the most modern and expensive lodgings in town.

5) Arrive supplied with specific names of inexpensive places to stay, garnered from prior reading and compatriots. Jot down hints when given. One inexpensive lodging leads to another as you meet travelers who've passed through your destinations.

When disembarking, be able to pronounce choices in order of preference. Immigration authorities in tightly controlled countries eye you less apprehensively if you can rattle off where you'll be staying. Agents from expensive hotels leave you in peace. Also inquire about location of your choice before local private transporters converge.

6) Arriving without a lead, seek information from those who'll accept you as a budget traveler. In Europe check by the nearest beauty parlor or tavern. In Africa and Asia request a "least expensive place" when immigration officials ask your address. Taxi drivers may be helpful, but have more to gain in commissions and runaround rides. You could wind up at the end of a skimble-skamble paying twice the going rate for an inferior room. In Siem Reap, Cambodia, we playfully pitted one pedicab driver against another, promising to hire the one who recommended the cheapest hotel. Our sweepstake was an 80-cent double in an inn hidden away in the most convenient part of town.

7) Where there's a choice, don't rush to get settled. Check the knapsack and enjoy leisurely orientation wandering, incidentally noting hotels, comparing rates. Then pick up the bag.

8) Plan transportation towards a balance between the venturesome and the secure, the penurious versus the luxurious. Less picturesque stretches can be traveled at night. European hotel problems have been solved with a Eurail pass. Deck passage for a few days offers a budget breather. With arrivals or departures during the wee hours, join the town and skip an unnecessary night's bunk bill. On stretches where routing is via IATA carriers, the airline picks up the tab on hotel and

food until the next onward flight to the place listed on your ticket. If infrequent schedules permit you a night or two in town, why not plan on it?

9) Finally, maintain a balance which preserves not only the health of your budget, but of yourself. Marginal facilities add spice and memories to an odyssey constantly extended by the savings thus generated. But an unbroken diet of any one thing spells trouble.

NON-HOTELS

Government facilities run from those designed for visitors to those maintained for the convenience of the state, but available to wayfarers. Some are located in game parks and ancient cities; others in places where your arrival causes ripples in the backwaters. A few may be available only in an "emergency."

Plentiful and reliable for backpacking nomads are government rest houses and Dak bungalows, found throughout the former British world: East Africa, Malaya, and particularly India, Ceylon, and Pakistan. They range from mansions surrounded by gum trees and parrots to stone chalets and flowered English cottages. From Himalayas to Sundarbans, putting up for just over 25 cents, you'll find them everywhere you go.

Railroad stations throughout India have overnight facilities with baths, known as "retiring rooms." For a few rupees and a ticket for a concluded or beginning journey, you may sleep up to 24 hours. Those not inclined to splurge under these tempting circumstances find railway bench sleeping acceptable anywhere in India. Free benches plus showers and all the basic amenities are offered in station waiting rooms, from first class through second, interclass (a face-saving label for third), and even third class, depending on the traveler's ticket.

Government accommodations normally available when others are tight, are military or police installations, including military guest rooms, officers' quarters, and barracks. For maximum safety when stuck, you may go to the police, who'll find you a union hall, courtroom table, or celebrity cell.

National parks' facilities in southern Africa and Japan, as well as the U.S.S.R. when traveling by road, add rare luxury to what's loosely referred to as "camping." Cottages come equipped with showers and firewood. Complete meals are available, and abundantly stocked commissaries sell or rent items not provided.

Religious organizations sometimes run inexpensive hostelries. The farther one wanders, the more prominent missions become. A contribution at leavetaking repays, in some measure, the hospitality. Sikh temples offer free room and board to all wayfarers as an essential of their religion. Their Golden Temple at Amritsar, India, maintains elaborate guest rooms. Hindu temples throughout the East also welcome any and all, but come equipped with sleeping bag. Buddhist monks frequently invite English-speaking visitors. Mission hotels in Denmark provide immaculate, inexpensive lodging. Worldwide services of the Salvation Army are sometimes geared to the budget tourist along with visiting missionaries. India's Red Shield Houses charge about $1.50 per day, including meals.

Spirit, not age, is your passport to acceptance in most youth hostels scattered throughout the world, Switzerland excepted. In Europe hostels are usually found within a comfortable day's walking distance from each other. A European-bound passholder can put up in Rome's former Olympic quarters, Swiss ski lodges, French abbeys, English town houses, German castles, and aboard a Swedish square-rigger. Knapsack toters with American Youth Hostel membership can choose from 250,000 beds available in 4000 hostels throughout 38 countries.

Hostel fees are negligible and you save by cooking. Sometimes the setup is completely informal. You could be on your own. Other hostels are strongly organized. The Hald International Student Center in Viborg, Denmark, for example, offers communal meals, frequent lectures, organized recreation and sightseeing tours for about $2 a day. Don't draw conclusions from a limited sampling of hostels. There'll be times when you'll be wiser to make for the nearest hotel. But overall experience, with restorative swapping of tales and information, especially off-season, should be good.

Student hotels, as opposed to youth hostels, are found throughout Europe and a number of other areas. While the rates are higher (European average: $1.25 per night), facilities are superior. Student credentials are usually necessary.

Universities frequently have inexpensive (occasionally free) facilities for traveling students, and the most priceworthy meals anywhere. Major cities sometimes have non-profit accommodations for students.

U.S. Peace Corps hostels are located in the main cities of developing countries. Summarized in order of priority, the residences are set up for 1) present Peace Corps Volunteers on business or vacation; 2) former PCV's; 3) U.S. travelers; and 4) others. The non-PCV pays approximately $.50, which includes bedding. You may cook your own meals or chip in with others.

One advantage of staying at a Peace Corps hostel is the fresh breeze of people you'll meet. They'll know more of the things you'll want to know than anyone else, and can fill you in on unusual spots and inexpensive travel around neighboring countries. To visit with them in their own locales is the quickest way to know the "real country." That dried soup or chocolate you've toted from home may find an appreciative "fish and loaves" ending here. Peace Corps hosts eagerly share and pump you of travel ideas. Many plan to make the homeward trek the long way, and prepare with adventurous trips within leave's distance of their assignment areas.

Small family hotels, boarding houses, and pensions take a more personal interest, give a flavor of the country, and are much less expensive than their overgrown relatives. In Europe they tend to cluster within a short radius of the railroad station. Pensions offer meals. "Half Pension" consists of room, breakfast and dinner; "Full Pension" includes all meals. Myriad Japanese inns line that country's side streets. Throughout Southeast Asia small, extremely clean, and inexpensive hotels are found in the Chinese quarters of town.

YM-YWCA's are identified by the triangle, since their letters differ. Many, such as the Chinese YMCA in Singapore, accommodate both sexes. The Hong Kong "Y" has inexpensive rooms, and one of the best roof-garden views of the city. Crossroads dormitories, as in Jordanian Jerusalem or Istanbul, are nightly treasure chests offering the rarest gems of onward travel tips.

Paying guest accommodations in Europe, and often elsewhere, are run at non-hotel prices by people who've been left with something bigger than their incomes. They range from the extremely inexpensive to the aristocratically unique, including converted European castles and maharajah's palaces. You can also stay in hunting lodges, hill and oasis way stations, and even trees. Nepal and Hawaii have variations on Kenya's famous "Treetops." Petra has its "tombs."

Israel's kibbutzim offer inexpensive, sometimes free, accommodations. Make arrangements through the Israel Student Association, or Histours in Jerusalem, Tel Aviv, or Haifa.

When traveling by plane, IATA airlines will teletype ahead for hotel bookings. Insist on the least expensive. You're not bound by what they arrange. Accommodation services, provided at many airports, sometimes take the budget tourist under their wing.

For extended stays, villas and cottages rent for a mere pittance compared to costs at home. These may be shared. Specifics on rentals in Mexico, the West Indies, Europe, North Africa, and the Middle East may be obtained from stateside organizations, or more reasonably once abroad. Prices from this side start at $35 a week, servants included. Mountain cottages, formerly vacation homes of British officers, available for under $5.50 a month, stand vacant in hill resorts such as Gulmarg, Kashmir. It's also possible to swap homes with a U.S.-bound traveler through the Vacation Exchange Club of Manhattan.

Anyone going East, and not wanting to miss one of the Good Lord's very special places, will investigate houseboats in the Vale of Kashmir. Meals, tea and shikara service for two cost $4.60 per day. Without food it's under 25 cents.

Alpine huts and mountain inns, be they in the Alps, Himalayas, or elsewhere, offer reasonable lodging plus one very special dividend—sunsets. Meals, however, are best carried in your pack.

Visiting with friends, and friends of friends, may spark new highlights to your tour. It's no trick to depart from home with an overkill number of letters of introduction. Too often, however, unknown acquaintances of acquaintances turn out like most blind dates. So keep those "you must meet" names generously spaced en route. Let these visits be travel rather than budget-oriented.

There are very few places you can't put up with sleeping bag and, if necessary, poncho. Steady starlighters suggest spots that are inconspicuous. Requests for camping space are rarely refused. Often you'll be asked to bring your bag under the roof.

CHECKING IN

Perhaps the sight of the knapsack has already melted the barriers which could stand between you and a reasonably priced room, or every room is thirty cents. If so, you're all set. If not, a firm check-in procedure is the all-important step in assuring inexpensive lodging. Because an empty hotel room leads only to overhead for each unrented night, off-season asking prices are subject to bargaining. Lowest rates, reserved for local, not tourist, travelers are not openly listed.

Ask for a reasonable room, immediately followed up by the question, "And how much is that, please?" In response to the first offer, you reply, "Oh, no, we don't need air-conditioning." On the next quotation, "We mean without bath," keeping in mind that the best repaid steps of your trip may be those extra few past a few doors down the hall. You can always add, "No, we really don't care about the view."

A request for the rate sheet might reveal something overlooked. If the last quotation still seems a bit out of line, raised eyebrows or a soft whistle are universally understood. Indicate your willingness to adjust.

Somewhere along the steps of this playful routine you'll be accommodated. Ask about the annex, overflow accommodations, or a home in the neighborhood which welcomes occasional referrals. European farmhouses are frequently eager to host a passer-through.

Remember, your knapsack demonstrates not only your philosophy of travel but your mobility to walk to the next hotel should reasonable prices not be forthcoming.

Checking out, more often it's desk clerks of larger hotels who try to divert your pocket money into theirs. If you suspect you're being taken, ask to see the rate card, and insist on a receipt.

HOTEL CIRCUMVENTION

Predawn arrivals make the bench a popular target in the game of hotel circumvention. Although parts of Europe and the Far East are no longer so accustomed to bench nappers in waiting rooms, usually all you need do is find an unoccupied one. You may be asked to verify your status as a legitimate traveler, which is reassuring from the standpoint of safety. Station officials may even offer an empty carriage berth.

Easier to manage is hotel circumvention due to a late evening departure. Hotels will hold your bags long after checkout, or drop gear at terminus of departure. Then meander unencumbered, to make the most of the night life, often missed for activity-packed days, or a lingering dinner culled from the savings of another hotel skipped. When

fatigue threatens to overpower, settle in to catch up on correspond-
ence.

AND WHAT IF I'M STUCK?

You won't be. Simply adjust to something less than your hopes.
Every hotel, when booked, has alternatives to suggest, if you demon-
strate your flexibility. It may be in the help's quarters, with the
neighbors, in the manager's room, in a private beach cottage, in the
local barracks, on a well-stuffed couch in the darkened lobby, in the
hotel owner's family compound, or a cheaper hotel.

When called for, your sleeping bag and plastic sheet provide an
independence not afforded other travelers. Then any logical corner
that's safe and clean sees you through the night, from across a waiting
room bench to beside the embers of a herdsman's fire. But generally
local hostelries, often in the shadow of a prouder, listed establishment
charging ten times your own night's lodging, will provide, in addition
to atmosphere, the privacy and rest to continue your travels. Also
the funds.

CHAPTER 6

HOW TO STRETCH FOOD SUPPLIES

Foreign economies allow dime-to-dollar gourmet meals along with rolling your own. Your first meal abroad may cost less than the tip of your last at home.

EATING OUT

Knapsack campers used to preparing their own food will find it's easier to patronize eateries where they exist. Since most countries are agricultural, food, even when eaten out, can be your smallest travel expense.

"Bed and breakfast" is the rule in British-style inns. At off-beat hotels, and European pensions, find out if best value is full, half, or without board. Eating at a hotel is usually a mistake, unless it's the only place in town.

Good food is the rule where customers are local people. Check side streets first. Watch for restaurants with fixed price menus in the windows. Impressive printed menus warn of overhead and inflated style. Humble-appearing "French" establishments from Vientiane and Vietnam to Bamako and Burundi can be destructively expensive.

Patronize the self-service restaurants of working inhabitants. Behind the Iron Curtain, try the workers' cafeterias; in Britain, the working-men's pubs. Japanese one-dish meat and rice meals can be had for twenty-five cents. Oriental "Yum Cha's," meaning "drink tea," let you select from trays carried around by waiters. You pay by the number of empty baskets at meal's end. Morning Yum Cha specialities available for pennies include dumplings filled with shrimp, meat, or vegetables. Or eat lunch in a European grocery as you might in a delicatessen at home.

Look for restaurants clustered around markets, central squares, train and bus depots. Most do a volume repeat business, open early, and close late. That empty yearning can also be satisfied from selected stalls, vendors, counters, snack bars. Satay grills in Southeast Asia serve beef or pork with tangy sauce on palm-leaf skewers. The Middle East has shish kebab. Pakistani stands boast broiled-to-order lamb, tenderized in pepper and yogurt. Mexican tacos (meat- and vegetable-filled tortillas) and quesadillas (fish- or meat-filled, deep-fried sandwiches) cost about two cents. Mexican bakeries rival French and Italian, at lower prices.

When train stops reveal exotic goodies, it may be your only chance to taste regional delicacies at a pittance. Japanese railroad vendors sell wooden-boxed meals complete with chopsticks, and frozen mandarin oranges. South African stations have nickel hamburgers. Thai station vendors serve broiled chicken, shrimp puff pastry, and roast corn on the cob. Rollers-through in Southeast Asia can stop for a bowl of meat, noodle, and vegetable soup cooked, for a few pennies, before one's eyes. Bananas and oranges abound at most tropical stations. Others specialize in grilled meat on a skewer, unshelled peanuts, or delicious smoked fish. Nigerians peddle "penny chop," a one-shilling meat and rice dish. Indian depots sell hot tea and boiled milk in throw-away clay mugs. Meals consisting of curry to dessert may be ordered on Indian and Pakistani trains at one station, delivered at a second, and paid for with two rupees at the third.

BEING FLEXIBLE

Adjust mealtime habits to those of the country. Sometimes it's best to join the crowd in a big lunch, with a snack for supper. "Businessman" noon specials are best buys in large cities throughout the world.

But generally adopt a traveler's eating schedule. A solid breakfast and looked-forward-to dinner clear the day for active travel. In the tropics even two meals may seem too heavy. Most West Africans grab a running morning bite and wait until night to truly eat. Usually midday meals become snacks, then disappear entirely to conform to a knapsacker's schedule.

Eat a big breakfast. Moving eastward from British orgies with bacon and sausage, count on sweets and coffee, followed by crackly bread half as big as your knapsack. On, past the land of blintzes with strawberry jam, you next encounter sheet bread, boiled milk, fermented grape juice, yogurt, and honey. Coffee is taken separately at a coffee house, which is the neighborhood bar. Beyond the lands of curry, it's fried fish and shrimp. Pork and garlic soup leaves you at the edge of the Pacific, forever spoiled for corn flakes.

Extend elaborate meals an extra round by artful culling. Portable leftovers provide manna for dawn departures, or where tea is served with rising.

Health and vigor can also be inexpensively maintained by scrapping ideas of "balanced" meals for meatless varieties. Much of the world is vegetarian, and milk and wheat are not staples in the Orient. You can manage, if you wish, on fresh fruits, vegetables, nuts. Natural meals are not only healthful and economical, but easily carried and require no cooking.

Cut the cord with Western menus. Their all too familiar prices should encourage weaning from taste prejudices early along the knapsack path. Adjustments occur more readily when you're hungry. In much of Africa, Latin America, and West Asia, the hotter the country, the hotter its food. An accompanying beverage will help your tongue survive until it adjusts. French and Chinese meals rate highest praise. While the French is usually overpriced, Chinese food is always a bargain.

You can point, in any native eating house, to what looks good on a nearby table. Or order from a trip to the kitchen. Some places exhibit sample platters marked by numbers. Desired quantities of ready-to-serve foods can be indicated by holding up how many fingers' worth you wish. Rice is a regular side dish through most of Asia, as is bread in the West.

Apart from providing budget sustenance, eating local adds variety to your travels. Towels, steamed or refreshingly icy, are served with many Eastern meals. In Bali you may eat spirit offerings if you first toss petals three times, then fold hands in prayer. Chinese meals, cooked to order so that bacteria have no time to form, can be tackled by a team. Middle Eastern cooking goes heavy on mutton, peppers, nuts, and fruits. Turkey has dolma, shashlik, and kofte. Israel, scarce on bagels and lox, leans on Turkish fare. Hindus like vegetables. Moslems skip pork. Certain Singapore restaurants serve girls with their food. Japanese meals can be a palette of plates. The simplest ryokan meal is laid out in twenty or more tiny dishes like point and counterpoint.

You'll become adept at eating with chopsticks, pointed sticks, Persian bread, tortillas, chapatis, banana leaves, foufou, and fingers. Chopsticks are limited to Japan, Korea, Taiwan, Hong Kong, plus Chinese restaurants elsewhere. Neighboring Orientals play variations on a silverware theme. Leaving a fork up can mean you want more meat; forget to place spoon downward, you're loaded with more rice. Moslem eaters use the right hand only. To avoid offending, pass, receive, eat, also pour drinks, pay tips, and fares with the dexter side. Before self-consciously spoon-twisting spaghetti, notice the Italians round you stuffing it in all ends dragging.

Knapsackers find frequent opportunities for pitching in or sharing meals. Fellow passengers, fascinated by your unfamiliar larder, will offer from their own. The slaughter of a goat on your arrival, however, should be in your honor, not on your bill.

SPECIALIZING IN SPECIALITIES

In Bangui, Central African Republic, orange juice, coffee, and croissants comes to, in local terms, 770 bananas. Buying bananas in banana country prevents running out of funds before appetite. Fondu, minus the silver forks, is the cheapest meal when dipped with chunks of Alpine bread. Frogs' legs, considered worthless in Eastern Europe, are best overlooked in France, indulged in the Orient. Overseas chicken, usually scrawny, can never be so delicious, or so cheap, as at home.

Stick to foods in season. In mango time, that's the delicacy to eat and eat. Oranges, even in orange country, should be forbidden fruit with off-season prices up to thirty times the usual going rate.

Avoid imports. Chocolate and apples should be taboo in the Punjab as might be litchi nuts and papayas in England. Three dollars buys a bottle of familiar beer in Mali, versus ten cents for good African palm wine, or local brew. A three-dollar shot of Scotch in Spain makes as much sense as a Spanish Fundador brandy in a Scottish pub. Better to tap a Spanish café's row of wine kegs at a penny or two per glass. Specialize in local specialities, including restaurant specials of the day.

ROLLING YOUR OWN LUNCH

Traditional knapsack cooking gear is better left at home. But a compact supply of food, drink, and light utensils is sometimes essential while on the road. On trains dipping behind the Iron Curtain (to Moscow is three days), you could go hungry until cashing in pre-purchased tourist coupons. Even if you're more inclined towards eating out than mess-kitting around, there'll be times when your ingenuity is taxed to find inexpensive meals. Pots of groundnut stew simmer before family rondavels, but nowhere is there a pot, or beanery for you.

You can fast, then feast. Or stock up at the market. At minimum there'll be the regional version of bread and fruit. Market fruits range from melons to dates, papayas, mandarins, mangosteens, rambutans, guavas, loquats, figs, mangoes, custard apples, and tree tomatoes. Green coconuts offer delicious jelly as well as juice. When you buy a dozen oranges to the accompaniment of giggles, they could be lemons. Ignore Latin giggles on bananas. The "horse fodder" type is what you want. "Regulars" go into the frying pan and come out tasting like potatoes. Don't buy ready-to-eat fruits; peel your own.

As insurance against late night arrivals and scalpers, carry a few non-perishables such as a can of meat or tube of cheese, replenishing along the way. A tasty British-made jar of Marmite (brand name) stretches indefinitely, converting bread to sandwiches or boiling water to soup. A salt and pepper mixture enhances tomato, avocado, and other vegetable combos. Immersion heaters create tea, bouillon, cocoa, coffee, packet soups for a private meal in your room.

Knapsack travels may be interspersed with camping out, hostelling, and picnic opportunities to brew potluck. A handful of market produce becomes an inexpensive stick-to-your-ribs stew. An Alaskan funds and stomach stretcher combines 1) some bacon, 2) more onions, and 3) loads of potatoes, fried crispy brown.

Extensive reliance on your own services warrants carrying a single aluminum pot and collapsible stove. Auto campers may heat canned foods on the engine while driving, with dinner at the next attractive view. Hotel hot water taps are mildly useful in a pinch.

Middle Eastern travelers literally roll their own lunch in Arabian envelope bread. Stuffings of broiled meat, eggs, honey, chopped vegetables, fish, lentils, olive oil can be self-administered, or injected by vendors.

69

Comparison shopping in the dusty bazaars of the Middle East, the crowded stalls of Japan, Taiwan, Indonesia, or the vivid plazas of Central and Latin America can be rewarding if you shop as do housewives everywhere, for value. The better you bargain, the better you eat. Silence Vesuvian rumblings, take your time, and prices begin to accommodate the sagging money belt. A stand of genuine rejection can leave you laden with provisions for yourself and the neighbors as well.

Watch a few transactions. See how much is being paid. Then decisively offer the same. Prices tend to go down with the sun.

From Scandinavian smorgasbord to Bangkok's floating market and Aberdeen's floating restaurants, you can graciously eat your way around the world without breaking your budget. The name-dropping delights of others will become your favorite budget stretchers. A recipe of a favorite dish is a good-for-a-lifetime souvenir. And it's duty-free.

CHAPTER 7

TIPS ON SEEING AND DOING

Knapsackers content with rushing from city to city, with detached views of the world through moving windows, might as well be on a 21-day globe-girdling idiodyssey. Ambitious overviews gobble funds and buy stock impressions for what might have been insights. Highlight surveys covering a compendium of world's-fare possibilities needn't be superficial when planned to include periodic experiences in depth.

Select key areas for special attention. What's closely studied in one place applies broadly to its neighbors. Concentration on the best representative example converts running around to seeing and doing. Longer stays also reduce daily costs. Distinguish between depth and overfocus. Paris can be as broadening as any city, but one who makes it his total experience can still return an international ignoramus.

BUDGET HAVENS VS. TRAPS

The more popular a country with tourists, the more expensive it becomes—for tourists. Today's most inexpensive countries include:

Latin America	Europe	Africa	Asia
Guatemala	Greece	Algeria	India
Ecuador	Yugoslavia	Congo	Pakistan
Peru	Spain	Ethiopia	Indonesia
Mexico	Austria	South Africa	Nepal
Most others	Turkey		Afghanistan

Economies change, but destined to continue on the expensive side are France, Switzerland, Sweden, West Africa, the West Indies, Venezuela, Japan, and individually guided Iron Curtain tours (Soviet tourist-class group tours are reasonable). But Switzerland offers fine rooms for $1.25; Sweden and Japan have $2 doubles, and these countries are bargains in terms of value. Israel, a most expensive Eastern country, is a least expensive Western one. Factors relative to the size of a country's bite are: 1) your amount of hopping about; 2) acquaintances there; 3) activities choices; and 4) the currency situation. Knapsackers sometimes find their first countries "expensive," their final ones "real bargains"!

Concentrate on less expensive places with the same features. Austrian Alps are cheaper than Swiss. The Mediterranean can be enjoyed in Spain, Yugoslavia, North Africa, and Turkey as delightfully as on France's Riviera. Acapulco's neighbors are "undiscovered" seaside villages. A three-cent ferry ride transports you from Hong Kong's expensive hotels to equally comfortable Kowloon ones.

Don't linger in the cities. Urban dollars are worth two in countryside rambling. Go one step beyond the usual. All too frequently, travelers draw financial limits just before the finish line. That extra effort, having come 99 per cent of the way, opens the new, the more significant.

Beware the circuit approach of tourists trying to "do" a country. One-night stands broken by daily transportation can leave you financially as well as physically exhausted. Find an inexpensive base. Park. Work from there.

Don't be discouraged by the expensive reputation of any longed-for spot. A knapsacker's means for short-circuiting conventional drains are adequate to the most advanced tourist-plucking conspiracies. Since knapsack travelers stay tuned to the native economy, no country is inaccessibly expensive.

LET INTERESTS DETERMINE DESTINATIONS

The knapsack jet-set go-goes somewhere worthwhile. Are you relaxation/contemplation-motivated? Escapist islands and bypassed budget corners invite a different pace. Are you study/subject-directed? Music festivals, empires' ruins, unprobed villages, galleries of the world await. Sports-minded? Include firstrate spots for skiing, skin diving, fishing, sailing, surfing, riding, or hunting. Professionally concerned? Visit comparable businesses, schools, government institutions. Artistically inclined? Uncork dreams for sketching, photography, writing, first-hand drama, new music, folk arts. Action oriented? Many service

74

programs welcome your help. Fortune seeking? Underdeveloped corners have mineral boom towns, undermarketed wares, and reputable businessmen looking for a representative in the American market.

Tokyo, Tahiti, the Riviera entice lively tastes. India's temples, Kyoto's shrines, Ba'albek, Katmandu, Jerusalem, invite religious comparisons. Pompeii, Fatehpur Sikri, Angkor Wat, the Hermitage, Luxor, and the Louvre, reveal man at his creative best. Verdun's trenches, Normandy's beaches, Auschwitz, Hiroshima, the Berlin Wall, speak to modern issues.

Beachcomb. Trek. Camp. Ride a canal boat. Retrace Biblical steps. Peek into a volcano. Sleep in a ghost town. Pub-hop. Visit a mine. Drop a dollar at the casino. Join an industrial shop tour. Comb the casbah, or an old foundation, for coins. Take in the world's great glockenspiels! Knapsackers shouldn't miss any once-in-a-lifetime chance to indulge that interest, hobby, or just plain whim. Whatever your cup of travel tea, allow for drinking deeply.

Let curiosity make you a firsthand participant. Instead of marching herd fashion through Munich's Hofbrau Haus, stop by at night for a beer with Bavarians. Visit a mosque or Buddhist temple for services; a church during wedding or choir rehearsal; understand the burning ghats of Benares and Calcutta as a solemn funeral participant. Tramp the fields of Ardennes with a veteran. Climb the Eiffel Tower. The pyramids of Gizeh are best appreciated from the back of a camel, from within their inner tombs, and from a view off the top. Many archeological sites invite not only looking, but digging. Pericles reads best in the columned shadows of the Parthenon. Absorb monastery life with a monk. Enjoy festivals with celebrants. Join the bustle of central markets as a buyer. The Paris Opera looks better with music. Arab, Laotian, Tibetan refugee camps are grateful for a helping hand.

GETTING ORIENTED

Check government tourist offices at ports of entry for maps, literature, and free services. Reviewing your accumulated notes against map, coordinate objectives with public transportation. Then, leaving the knapsack behind, walk. Increasing familiarity leads logically to further destinations within a city, and then beyond.

Being slightly ahead in your reading saves you time, money, and frustrations that otherwise prevent getting the feel and full enjoyment of a place when you most need it—at arrival.

Many of life's luxuries are free, yours for the seeing. Much that's abroad becomes increasingly like what's at home. Spend your time with the unique.

Be selective. Would you eat everything on a menu? Absorb, digest, and enjoy, or suffer an upset above the stomach. Travel poster spots are often thronged. Go mornings, before arrival of sightseeing busses and hawkers. Many museums and shrines have free days, commonly Sundays. Monuments represent the past, and rarely stack up to dynamic human institutions of the present. Balance your sights for their usefulness in cutting through the greater human story.

Go open-minded, your antennae tuned to small newspaper items, overheard comments, ideas hidden in novels as well as guides. Jot down future leads in your private-eye notebook. Don't be trapped into compulsive sightseeing. Let the feelings generated mingle with your other thoughts. Move as the spirit moves. If you don't like a place, it's a big world; move on.

WHEN TO USE TOURS AND GUIDES

Most are a tourist crutch not needed by knapsackers. Blanket rejections, however, cut you out of intriguing situations, including covert religious rites, family celebrations, and institutions purposely overlooked by the official tourist office.

A guide, where you need one most, is affordable, usually under a dollar a day, and should be considered when 1) an activity is closed to the lone outsider, 2) he's capable of meeting your interests, 3) it seems as if you'll enjoy his company, and 4) fee, in keeping with local wages, is established in advance.

Let a guide talk you into his services, giving you a chance to assess his English, honesty, experience, credentials, and fee, and only *after* your own wanderings confirm need. Residents, a new acquaintance, and students eager to practice English may also take you below the surface.

Tours should be considered if they provide cheapest transportation, or overview understanding for personal followup. They can also introduce companionship. Don't get booked in advance. Standard U.S.

fees (typically $10) are, for the same tour, fractional locally. In most cases the collective is not for you, but be sure.

ZEST THROUGH PACING

Alternate travel with rest, hard going with idle loafing. Repeated routines require injections of variety. Restoratives and a periodic splurge are needed to maintain curiosity as well as vigor.

Supplement garden meals with hot, occasional Western ones. Periodic settling in along the way, in spots intriguing and inexpensive, makes possible becoming part of local routines. Laundry, letters, loose ends can be handled. Also relax, and let yourself reflect on your own life activities.

A traveling pace starts early in the day. Listlessness is sometimes traced to throwing off too many former habits, like starting the day briskly.

Arriving at a new place, rest before going out. Enjoy the place you've come these many miles to know.

Spend weekends as at home. Sundays, not observed in many places, should be kept easy and to your inclinations.

OFF-BEAT IS "IN"

Knapsack lets you duck behind the new facades for easier travel within the most colorful, least expensive places on earth. Save some countries for those creaky years; those dark and mysterious corners out of travel lore, now jet-hitched to the 20th century, should be visited before they take on its trappings.

River boats connect jet ports with the aborigines. Busses drive where game roams freely and sorcery is widely practiced. Light planes fly into Australian and New Guinea clearings surrounded by the Stone Age. Timbuktu becomes a starting base, rather than an expedition goal. Polynesian islands, time-sealed valleys, even the edges of Everest and Antarctica are opened to the tourist.

Explore Incan ruins. Ski in Swat. Visit Devil's Island. Safari independently in East Africa. Schooner cruise South Pacific islands. Dive on the Great Barrier Reef, or among Caribbean hulks. Trek in Nepal, Guatemala, Ethiopia, Japan, or less populated lands where major discoveries await—Australia's Outback, Mexico's Yucatan (south of our border there's knapsack challenge equal to any further afield), tributaries of the Amazon and Congo, Alaska.

The more difficult an area, the easier it is to knapsack. Assistance is volunteered by missionaries, government officials, and commercial exiles, delighted to meet a newcomer who's come "here, of all places."

GETTING ACROSS

A smile, gesture, broken phrase, being seen carrying your own knapsack out beyond the satellite hotels—these are the knapsacker's people-to-people passkeys to the main arena. An African goatherd, pointing to his skin, asks, "America, liberté? Fraternite? Non." "Oui," you reply, and share a communal meal. Gestures, away from the international watering holes, speak louder than feeble phrases. Uninhibited pantomime helps.

People provide places with the indispensable dimension of life. To know travel's richest afterglow you needn't be especially conspicuous, gregarious, or multilingual—just interested. A wilderness priest needs intellectual stimulation, and tobacco; islanders an excuse for a party. Exiles long for company. Teenagers read you as their plug-in to the latest. Students cheer a chance to practice English. Communists eye a potential convert. Energetic hosts enhance their prestige with you as a guest. Your mere presence may assure a merchant a more decent commission or a traveling companion better treatment as you cross what for him is an unfriendly border.

BREAKING THROUGH THE LANGUAGE BARRIER

English is spoken in all the places where the sun never used to set, and, by a minority, in the most unlikely spots. A second language, or smidgen-pidgin, or picked-up-on-the-run phrases are helpful. Then there's sign language, drawing in the sand, and pantomime, which don't add up to conversation, but adequate communication.

Your first day or two out of the country may be strained. Then, through an unconscious process which heightens reliance on powers of observation, language problems fade. Clues from tone of voice, facial expressions, and gestures within limits of anticipated response, also help point to the answer. In a very few days you pick up enough of the crucial phrases to slip by.

MEETING PEOPLE COMES NATURALLY

An air of friendliness abroad brings many takers. It makes you, the usually inaccessible foreigner, approachable. The quickest way to meet someone in town is to pull out a map. From the friendly advice which immediately gathers, someone's going your way, with a chain reaction that can go on for days. Selection of your seat companion, and choice of lodging can also open local doors. Talk to strangers. Ask questions. Showing interest in children breaks the ice with mamma and papa.

Having a specialized travel goal puts you in purpose-related contact with residents. USIS promotes gatherings for contact between natives and visitors. Visitors to local meetings of familiar organizations are welcome guests. Even Katmandu has a Kiwanis Club.

Occasional tieups with fellow knapsackers can lead to a program more adventurous than likely to be taken on alone. Avoid travelers whose endless comparisons of lodgings and food reveal limited success in getting beyond the mechanics of travel.

Urban sociability is more localized in cafés, parks, and in after-hours corners. Strummers and harmonicists carry a social vehicle, but "He that would make his travels delightful," Seneca tells us, "must first make himself delightful."

AVOIDING PEOPLE

The celebrity role wears thin quickly. There can be times when, the more the harrieder, you're not alone and might like to be. Short-lived bouts with loneliness become, more often, a growing desire for solitude.

Not looking like a tourist pays off in protective coloration. When manner blends with mores, you'll not be hounded. Hucksters and guides are encouraged when you show uneasiness. A firm "no," with continuing step is usually sufficient. To confuse your own feelings about the wretched existence of people with the false premise that politeness will work in dealing with a rogue is to be taken for a chump.

Children, always delightful, can be children. Sometimes playing pied piper can be fun, but generally mob scenes aren't easy to control, especially if there's rumor of a handout. Ignore advances, and your privacy will be respected.

LOCAL CUSTOMS, TIPPING

Broad leeway is granted travelers, who are assumed not to know a region's customs. Normal courtesy and respect sees you through. Sensitivity earns you points. Practice of newly learned customs can bring down the house.

Take cues from around you. You'll notice shorts are taboo in many countries, that women are sometimes expected to cover their heads or arms, that mosques and temples are trod without shoes. You won't be struck dead for inadvertently speaking to a woman in purdah; a middle ground between bashfulness and brashness will serve most needs.

Good news. Knapsackers aren't viewed as tippers. You may wish to, particularly those who depend on tips. Most locally patronized spots don't expect, or even know of, tipping. In some it could be insulting; in others you'll be chased, your "forgotten" coin returned. European hotel and food bills usually reflect a service charge. In Communist countries, tipping is out. In India you could tip a dozen times between the curb and your room, but needn't. Forget the guidebook rate tables. Play it by ear; be fair, and when necessary, make up the difference in friendliness.

VISITS IN HOMES

Joining a family around its glowing coals is heartwarming. Increasing numbers of government tourist offices will put you in contact with families. Other sources for prearranged contacts are U.S.-university foreign student advisors, foreign universities, groups like Servas Hospitality and American Friends of the Middle East, and overseas Americans.

While the affluent are quick on invitations, a typical host assumes his living standards aren't up to yours. His invitation, in spite of occasional inconveniences, is an unrefusable compliment.

COPING WITH BEGGARS AND POVERTY

Becoming blasé about poverty is an ostrich solution. But don't be bound by hopeless responses. You can't donate to every beggar.

Beyond the despair which overhangs parts of Latin America, Egypt, and a few other societies, people don't reflect a feeling of being poor, accepting their standard as the norm.

Only the traveler who feels disdain, or naive pity, is at their mercy. To steer clear of native quarters is a great mistake. When a situation finds you unsure of control, smile, give a wave, and, without a backward glance, walk slowly onward. Security is assured by maintaining your dignity, quite another thing from being heartless.

And still you'll give to beggars. With an orange to a ragged child, an onlooker whispers, "And there is the national wealth of our country." Seeing her run happily off, he adds, "Touching another soul is like touching the soul of all mankind."

But give judiciously. Or be besieged. Aggressive professionals like to badger and see you ruffled, but quickly sense experience in response. And serve as you wish, in any of your countrymen's numerous projects on behalf of all the world, upon your own informed return.

PHOTOGRAPHY

If you plan to photograph, keep camera always with you, on a shortened strap, under jacket, for easy, unobtrusive carrying and a fast draw. Best results require an awareness of 1) form (composition), 2) texture (lighting), and 3) mood (which calls for a conscious definition of human interest and why you want this picture).

Get close to your subject. Let it fill the entire lens. People are used to travelers carrying cameras, and usually like to be photographed; your manner of behavior makes it a compliment. Point to your camera, nod with a smile, shoot, wave and bow your thanks, then move on. This won't work so smoothly if you invite questions and doubt during awkward struggles with equipment. Fast shooting is important enough to practice at home, and further reason for leaving the accessories there. Be inconspicuous, respectful of cultural limits, display a confident manner, and you'll get all the pictures you want.

For candid shooting, 1) wait until you're no longer a novelty, or threat. Then shoot what you were after, or potluck on what develops. Or 2) point in a non-threatening direction. Then swing quickly, shooting what you want. 3) Park friend next to subject. Slight movement of the camera, left or right, gets subject, while your body remains inclined towards friend. 4) Scan. And scan and scan. Somewhere in your sweeping circles you click, but who knows where? 5) Carry camera preset for average light conditions and distance, shooting instantly, without missing a step, as subject presents itself.

It's possible to come home with representative photos made at no expense to seeing and doing, *if* you learn to shoot as naturally as you do everything else.

LIVING IT UP

Stalking local fun and affordable entertainment supplies night-on-the-town medicine for days around town. Overseas clubs are generally cheaper by American standards. Some night clubs, however, if you leave the bar for a table, are a convenient device for dropping whole countries from your trip.

Guidebooks, equating entertainment with night clubs, list spots in the fleshpot cities—Acapulco, Beirut, Hamburg, Hong Kong, Paris, Rotterdam, Saigon, Tokyo. But every city has its Sodom-Gomorrah corner. Your best guide is a student bent on demonstrating his backdoor savvy. Tequila, tanzfrauleins, talking drums, what's your cup of brew? Teahouses also qualify as wicked spots.

Potables are procurable in most but not all places. Duty-free $2.25 Scotch can cost $25 to $70 in Southwest Asia. Best prices are in free-port shops strategically distributed from Shannon to Tokyo, or on in-transit planes and ships. Bargains abound in regional brews, made of such things as palm sap or ginseng root. Drinking in Moslem countries goes against the faith, but seeing yours, they'll swear they're Buddhist. Worth trying once are kola nuts in Africa, and pan (with betel nut) in the Indian subcontinent.

THE WORLD IS A STAGE

Most cities have English-language newspapers which list events. Government tourist offices may steer you in special directions. More fruitful sometimes, question natives. More adventurous is to simply wander. There's no price of admission to the everyday fun and games of others.

Some of the best free shows are put on by traveling acts for super patent medicines. Wedding celebrations are another open-house favorite. In "poor man's night clubs," like the one in front of Hong Kong's Traffic Branch Police Headquarters, hawkers and fortune tellers hold forth while minstrels strum. Temple dances throughout Asia are usually free. Casinos require no more admission than a tie. You'll encounter festivals with wine running from fountains, dancing in the streets, and the far-gone laid out side by side to sleep it off. Annual independence days bring fireworks, folk dancing, corner orchestras, bonfires, pickled tink people in the trees, and sometimes a brand new revolution. Carnival time in Europe and Latin America and Japan's Bon Festivals find celebrating masses in a gigantic free show which you can join. Look for trade expositions with their rides, demonstrations, and window shopping exhibits. You'll stumble into free street operas, free-wheeling wine-tasting festivals, carnival-like markets, picnics with arm-swinging gemütlichkeit, church recitals, dance competitions, school programs, sporting events, British theatre (4 shillings), bull fights (4 pesos), cock fights, pachinko parlors, outdoor concerts, dedications, coming-of-age rituals, patriotic displays, political rallies, and zoos or botanical gardens, where you can listen to an orchestra, dance, play tennis, or dine.

Girls abound on Europe's beaches, men in the Alps, and perhaps you'd like to correct the imbalance. American clubs all over the world sponsor frequent social activities. American girls especially are never permitted boredom.

CONTACTS WITH HOME

The always close USIS library stocks American books and magazines. U.S. airlines offices carry the *New York Times.* International editions of *Time* and *Newsweek* blanket newsstands of the world. The company of AID, Peace Corps, military, and tourist Americans is there when you want it. Travel to the water cooler of your nearest U.S. consulate for reassuring affirmation of the existence of home. Then there are U.S. movies and ice cream, wherever you can find it pasteurized. The familiar is sometimes the knapsacker's best revitalizing diversion.

MOVIES

Even when relaxing, from box seats to dirt floor under thatch, with bicycle generator providing the juice, it's another new world at the movies. Watching audience often beats the screen. Try for the cheaper seats. They'll want to sell you something in the satin throne class, which may be just as well if you don't want to participate in the show.

SHOPPING AROUND

"Count your wealth not in having things, but in doing things. The wealthy are those who accomplish their desires." Shopping robs you of time, cuts into your budget, and therefore your itinerary. Toting is a tough proposition. Wrapping can be a half day's activity. Shipping is expensive, and the gauntlet may include half a dozen officials and twice that many forms. Then, assuming you're in a place where you can count on the postal service to get the precious wares back, you may find them at home for less than your purchase costs plus shipping.

If loved ones love you, they'll understand. Eating to stay healthy comes first. Getting to those once-in-a-lifetime corners, the ones, once you're almost there, which require that extra mile and another two dollars, that comes next.

Uncle Sam has done his bit to stretch your travel time and dollar by increasing import restrictions. But if you see something unique, that you can put to frequent use, or imagine as a treasure through the years, and you'll not have another crack at it, plunge. You'll still make it home.

Genuine antiques are duty-free, and bargains in certain cou ries. Duty-free ports are the place to get that permanent camera. And, if you can afford it, as your future reminder of other worlds and ways of doing things, that one-of-a-kind Hindu brass or African carving may be best engineered abroad, and now.

WHAT *NOT* TO BUY

Avoid purchases of anything that's 1) large, 2) heavy, 3) breakable, 4) perishable, 5) non-functional (except perhaps works of art), or 6) mass-produced (unless you need it now). Ignore cameras and watches from peddlars (cleverly spruced up, perhaps stolen), ivory (that's probably plastic), jade (that's probably not genuine or not legal—from Red China), or "antiques" from a hawker.

WHERE TO BUY

Avoid shops that cater to tourists for those serving repeat customers, such as department stores, markets, bazaars, or government emporiums, and, as in Japan, stores exempt from local taxes. Duty-free shops can be found aboard ships and at airports in Beirut, Cairo, Copenhagen, Karachi, Montreal, Paris, Shannon, Tel Aviv, Toronto, with more to open. Free ports include Macao, Panamá, Penang, Singapore, but the best are Aden and Hong Kong. Here, too, bargaining is the rule. At the outset you might consider camera, watch, trade goods, immediate gifts, and expendibles. En route stock up on film and replacement clothing. Home gifts are saved for the last oasis.

On purchases under $10, let the shop wrap and ship, if they'll guarantee safe delivery. Recent customs regulations place duty on more expensive items not personally carried. Smaller precious ones should stay with you. Know values. Shopping guides are unreliable, taking you to their friends for a commission.

BARGAINING

Haggling, i.e., doing business, can be dignified, or so, with a sense of humor, you should keep it.

Your strategy is trying to get a sense of the other fellow's position, arriving at a price near his preset minimum. Judge value by local standards. Know the currency. With interrupting pauses for mental calculations, you've already lost.

Tactics include: 1) pretending interest in something else; 2) making no offer, letting him set the price, then lopping it as a starter; 3) leaving, hoping to return if not stiff-armed at the door; 4) carrying a niggardly amount of money as all you can spend—coward!

Don't get discouraged. Practice. Learning the art could repay the cost of your trip when you later buy that home or business.

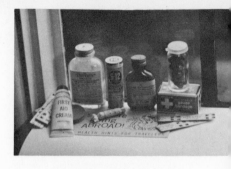

CHAPTER 8

STAYING SAFE, KEEPING FIT

Knapsacking is the safest form of adventure. Start your trip based on a faith in people, and you'll return reassured.

TIPTOEING THROUGH

Since Alabama and New York aren't off-limits because of racial and subway incidents, knapsacking abroad comes down to the same ground rules. Anti-American feelings? Your shouldered knapsack cuts down its basis. Aggressive nationalists are disarmed by your non-resemblance to their poster ideas of an imperialist war monger. We've visited, without incident, more than a score of countries undergoing growing pains, including war. The most foreboding place takes on warmth and charm as you get to know it.

Headlines don't necessarily mean trouble for you. A stone thrown in Johannesburg reverberates in the world press, but causes few local ripples. The people you'll meet wish to be allowed to work and live in peace. Even where travelers are allegedly unwelcome, their dollars aren't. In strife, both sides seek favor. In absolute danger, you won't find transportation or permits to get you there.

Carry your own knapsack for safety as well as economy. When your bag sits while you're doing something else, keep one foot pressed against its side. In transit, place it on an opposite, in-view rack. When sleeping, lie against it, or let it prop your feet. When you can't, don't worry. Fellow passengers look out for you. Don't leave passport, currency, tickets, camera in knapsack whenever you and it travel separately.

Keep your ears open to the reputation of a place. You have no worries in countries like Japan, but sections of Africa and Latin America require normal alertness. In the event of a problem--financial, accident, illness--call the U.S. (British, Canadian) consulate. Local police are sometimes better avoided, except on the advice of a responsible citizen. In trouble spots, sign in at American consulates at arrival. If comments like "bon courage" leap up from the register, discuss your plans with a consular representative.

Be cautiously open in police states. With good intentions you've nothing to fear, but why tempt reaction? When you enter a doubtful situation, have a second person with you, or your alternatives fixed in advance. Should someone seek trouble, smile back vacantly. You just don't understand. Be pleasant, don't telegraph your alarm, turn casually, and walk away. Remember, as do potential antagonists, you're represented by a powerful, and interested, government.

Every off-beat traveler is considered a writer, and you may, in difficulty, wish to perpetuate the illusion. A press card could be your trump card.

Be wary of gifts for delivery to strangers. When hitchhiking, you're not apt to ride with anyone doubtful. Don't avoid crowds, but mingle with reserve. When you become the center of too much attention, walk on. Protective coloration is achieved by behavior as much as costume. And don't let these precautions discourage you. Knapsacking is the friendly way to travel.

HANDLING MONEY

Travel's pleasures shouldn't be undercut by worry, which is the best case for using travelers' checks. Because one loses on their purchase, sometimes again at cashing, and accompanying services *don't* broadly cover the world, you may prefer carrying currency. On long trips you can periodically replenish your supply through conventional savings account withdrawals, converting mailed cashiers' checks into American dollars en route. A surprising number of places in primarily Western countries honor a personal check, or you can draw against a letter of credit.

A functional leather belt, with zippered lining, unobtrusively carries up to 20 bills. Available from Hammacher Schlemmer, 145 E. 57th St., New York, N.Y. 10022, is a 1 1/4" black or brown 2-zipper cowhide belt for $7.95. Spencer Gifts, Spencer Building, Atlantic City, N.J. 80404, carry one for $2.98. For girls they stock a bra bank, $1.00, as does Breck's of Boston, 300 Breck Building, Boston, Mass. 02210, which also sells a zipper-pocketed money garter for $1.00.

Your spare tire is a fifty- or hundred-dollar bill, put aside from regular cash. Should opportunity or emergency remind you of its presence, replace it as quickly as possible, safely out of sight. Don't leave a country stuck with large amounts of probably undervalued paper. A supply of five- and one-dollar bills can save last-minute transactions with larger denominations. Remaining coins at points of exit keep you in blades and toothpaste.

List expenditures in the back of your notebook. Besides providing an interesting record, it's your best control on overspending.

What happens if you're really down and out? The U.S. consulate, with more important things to do, will buy your passage directly home. It's a loan. Some travelers would rather give blood first, and do—at a good price.

CHANGING MONEY

Port of entry, airport, and hotel exchanges don't usually produce the best rate. Shop around, particularly where unofficial exchanges are the rule.

When money merchants block traffic around the national bank, or when they're permitted to mill in the government tourist office under a sign which reads: "All currency must be exchanged with an authorized representative at the official rate of exchange," you resent being held to an artificially pegged rate no longer respected by officials. When a banker with whom you intend a legitimate exchange dispatches a teller to lead you to more advantageous traders in the market, you may wish to play the new game. Play it by ear. Underdeveloped countries desperately need foreign exchange, a need with which you'll be in sympathy. But when cynical governments unfairly exploit the traveler, don't—unless you can afford $5 soup in Brazzaville, or a $64 room in Djakarta—curtail your trader's instinct to even the balance. Unenforceable currency declaration forms at entry are sporadically collected at departure, but should show a balance between amounts brought in and amounts exchanged. Travelers' checks are frequently not considered money. *Newsweek*'s international edition prints weekly summaries of true currency values. By comparing notes with travelers, and ignoring first offers of shopkeepers, you'll frequently do much better.

CUSTOMS AND IMMIGRATION FORMALITIES

Passport entries which once read: "Warned to report to police compound within 24 hours" now say: "Please visit the tourist office." Airport baggage checks have become a matter of minutes, with bag searches rare. Be prepared, with documents open, to justify unusual equipment or quantities. Show readiness to open knapsack, but reveal contents only as asked.

Calmly stand your ground if a customs man creates problems. He's looking for "dash," "baksheesh," a payoff. Liquor seems the traditional lubricant, but asking to see the chief inspector is easier. British inspectors, with authority to tax anything, can be easily ruffled, but are honest. European border crossings by train are often without any customs or immigration formalities. Soviet inspectors ask, "Have you any fruit or flowers?", and search not baggage but under the bunks and between carriage wheels. Latin border authorities may cause delays to justify "overtime" payments. Here it pays to be with a respected citizen, or first in line.

Our knapsacks have been emptied but once, and only because a rival accused our bus driver of smuggling gold. Pocket contents, including tear-gas pen, have never been noted.

Overland crossings, used by locals, tend towards greater fussiness. Back-country customs thugs are not above taking "gifts" of tribute from local passengers, but a tourist in these surroundings is respected, left alone. Most border authorities will bend in your favor, steer you to reliable lodgings, often invite you for coffee or tea.

U.S. customs usually ask returnees to open their bags. Get a free copy of *Custom Hints* at departure. You can bring home any amount of goods, of which $100 is duty-exempt. Those not accompanying you at return are charged at the usual rate, but you can send home daily, non-reportable, gifts under $10, true antiques, and anything you no longer need, duty-free. Regulations from U.S. possessions are more liberal. Goods from banned countries (Cuba, Communist China, North Vietnam, and North Korea) are prohibited. Save sales slips.

UNPREDICTABLES

Remember the joke about the marvels of jet travel ("Breakfast in Beirut, lunch in London, and baggage in Buenos Aires")? You'll encounter your share of unpredictables. Chalk it up to spice.

Sometimes your mind is cluttered with details, new requests, and your biggest danger is loss, not theft. Establish a definite routine and place for everything, and never show your money. Most of your transactions will be with fair, honest people, but any insurance company can write you a policy against losses. Should you bother, make sure it's truly comprehensive. Auto insurance can be a serious drain, $88 a month, for example, on the southern Pan American Highway.

GETTING PHOTOS AND GETTING THEM HOME

Resentments from exposure of a camera won't develop when you're smooth, natural, and quick. Don't penalize yourself by assuming resentments where they don't exist. Should a candid shot create a reaction of doubt, give your friendly wave and move on quickly. You'll see tourist-types hounded for tips simply because of their lingering "Gee, what a shot!" gloating expression.

To send films out, a few countries require censor's certification. Travelers have also reported damage from X-raying and exposed film pulled from canisters. Simply hold yours for periodic shipment home from reliable places.

PREDEPARTURE HEALTH PRECAUTIONS

Travel fitness begins with pretrip conditioning and inoculations. Start shots early, particularly if yellow fever, cholera, typhus, and typhoid are needed. A gamma globulin inoculation provides 6-month protection against hepatitis. Portable health preservers for your tiny kit include: Diaprin or Aralen tablets (weekly malaria preventatives); Enterovioform, or similar tablets (for diarrhea); sulfaguanidine, or some other prescribed antibiotic (for dysentery); aspirin or Empirin; band-aids; and snakebite kit. Drugs are far less expensive overseas, but you'll want to start out somewhat stocked, and O.K.'d by your dentist.

Most group insurance plans, such as Blue Cross and Blue Shield, can be continued on your own, and will cover medical costs incurred anywhere. Companies like Mutual of Omaha carry additional tailored plans. If you have a special medical problem, Intermedic, Inc. (777 Third Ave., New York, N.Y.) provides, for a membership fee of $5, a directory of English-speaking physicians in 75 foreign cities, listing phone numbers and fees.

Travel is physical. If vestigial legs need limbering, walk more at home. Substitute stairs for elevators, shoe leather for cabs. The totally spent might board a slow freighter to that first destination.

ON-THE-ROAD FITNESS

Excitement, worry, and overeating are major causes of motion sickness, and mental diversion one of several moderating devices. Stewardesses and pursers carry Dramamine, and you might keep some in your kit. Fresh air and calm provide relief without the sleepiness left by pills.

Staying active and in good spirits, eating sufficiently, and getting enough rest keep resistance high. One hot meal a day helps the morale, but isn't necessary to keeping fit. Morale itself affects the operation of your digestive tract, and maintains resistance. Non-air-conditioned accommodations are not only cheaper, but help you acclimatize to surroundings for overall health as well as comfort.

Remember preventatives. Antimalaria pills, taken weekly, should be tied with some bench-mark time, like Saturday nights. Advance-mark your notebook for en route booster shots (usually free). Travelers with forged health certificates, easily accomplished, miss the whole point—a big one.

Ignore the tropical ways of mad dogs and Englishmen; use local solutions for overexertion, extra salt and siestas included. Walking and hitchhiking under the sun calls for a hat. If camping out, use a head net. Mosquito nets are standard in even the simplest hostelry.

Swimming is safe in most places you find others, but some inviting lakes, particularly in Africa, are infected with schistosomiasis (carried by snails) and, though the surroundings would lull you to thinking you were at home, crocodiles. Sultry climates are not for heavy meals, rare steaks, walking barefoot, or strenuous activity without following rest.

"FUNNY TUMMY"

Begin your international smorgasbord with moderation. Change, not impurity, is more frequently the culprit behind "funny tummy." Pure water now runs from the taps of most major cities, but wise knapsackers develop a taste for tea.

Don't be swayed by those who boast of eating everything. Your stomach overseas can stay as reliable as at home by avoiding unboiled milk, cream-filled pastries, honey-bucket salads, ice in drinks, and locally concocted beverages. Unboiled water isn't magically purified by liquor. Boiling is best, since neither acquired immunities nor purification tablets kill hepatitis germs.

Though general immunities develop quickly, count on occasional rumblings from below. Where the Yogi swallows eight yards of gauze, then pulls it up with all impurities, you have your pills. Enterovioform can accompany stomach-soothing foods. Papayas, bananas, and durian (jackfruit) are especially effective. A daily multiple-vitamin pill offsets dietary imbalance and increases energy. Otherwise, avoid hygiene neurosis.

FINDING MEDICAL HELP

In many European, African, and Asian countries medical attention is free, with private service also available. Excellent American and European mission hospitals also cover the back country.

U.S. consulates and military bases are prepared to handle emergencies and make referrals. Pharmacists know the local maladies, particularly intestinal. Most are local medical heroes. Any overseas American has already mapped out his medical route in time of need, which can be yours in an emergency.

A pretrip first-aid review is recommended, but all first aid stems from these fundamentals:

1) Stop bleeding (local pressure should be sufficient).
2) Treat shock (head lower than feet, clothing loosened, patient kept warm; use ammonia if available).
3) Maintain breathing (use artificial respiration as necessary).

OVER AND OUT

You've opened, and walked through, new doors. You've felt the miseries, joys, and common bonds of humanity, and experienced a fuller range of your own powers. You've found it's possible to be exquisitely attuned to the universe, and someone asks, "What were you running away from?"

The question is: "What are you moving towards?", but no matter. You can't duplicate for others what for you came only through reality. Your new wine pours into old bottles, but you may have to revise some previously held values.

Anyone who's had a chance to enjoy an extension of living through knapsacking, to experience the essential unity of life, will find some chafing in stepping back into that highly specialized harness. During the "re-entry crisis" sort out and test new ideas, keep up with overseas friends, pick up threads with the old, read, perhaps assist a group's overseas project, convert memories to action, and charge on towards expanded horizons. Translation of your new awareness into former routines puts you further down the road towards the most precious of all degrees—that Ph.D. in Life.

I 6
295